NAME THE COUNTRY STAR WHO WROTE AND RECORDED THE THEME FOR HER FIRST FILM. ALSO NAME THE FILM.

WHAT TWO KENNY ROGERS SONGS WERE THE BASIS FOR A MOVIE?

WHAT COUNTRY SINGER WAS ELECTED GOVERNOR OF LOUISIANA?

WHAT SINGER HAS A ROAD NAMED AFTER HIM?

THE CLAMPETT FAMILY ON THE *BEVERLY HILLBILLIES* TV SERIES WAS INTRODUCED BY WHAT ARTIST AND SONG?

See just how well you know your country music—match your memory against these puzzlers and many more guaranteed to set your mind strumming to the tune of—

THE COUNTRY MUSIC TRIVIA QUIZ BOOK

ANSWERS: 1. DOLLY PARTON, *9 TO 5* 2. "COWARD OF THE COUNTY" and "THE GAMBLER" 3. JIMMY DAVIS 4. JOHNNY CASH 5. LESTER FLATT AND EARL SCRUGGS and their "BALLAD OF JED CLAMPETT."

Quintessential Quiz Books from SIGNET

THE
COUNTRY
MUSIC
TRIVIA QUIZ BOOK

by
Dennis Hazzard

Ⓢ
A SIGNET BOOK
NEW AMERICAN LIBRARY
TIMES MIRROR

TO

My wife Vivian and our children Amy and Mark, who observed the gathering of the trivia for this book with curiosity and encouragement.

 SIGNET TRADEMARK REG. U.S. PAT. OFF. AND FOREIGN COUNTRIES
REGISTERED TRADEMARK—MARCA REGISTRADA
HECHO EN CHICAGO, U.S.A.

SIGNET, SIGNET CLASSICS, MENTOR, PLUME, MERIDIAN AND NAL BOOKS are published by The New American Library, Inc., 1633 Broadway, New York, New York 10019

First Printing, March, 1983

    1 2 3 4 5 6 7 8 9

PRINTED IN THE UNITED STATES OF AMERICA

PREFACE

It is tagged "the music of the 1980's" and the new "middle-of-the-road" music by those all-knowing people who put labels on everything from soup cans to super highways. Actually, it is just country music, a music that has been around for many years. For some unknown reason it seems to have taken several country-accented films and a mechanical bull to explode this music into the mainstream. Scan a radio dial and country music is there on more frequencies than ever before. Check the clothing racks of a department store for the western influence on fashions or see all the country stars on the TV talk shows. Yes, cousin, country music has arrived.

So it is with this "coming out of the closet" that this country music trivia book came to be. Those who have always enjoyed country music will find a pleasant nostalgia trip here. For newcomers to the "sound of country" it will be an opportunity to learn about country's roots and have fun with questions on recent country stars and trends.

Special thanks to George Evanko for his assistance, to Joel Whitburn and his "Record Research" books, and to the Country Music Association for its continuing efforts to recognize country music's finest artists through its awards program and hall of fame and museum.

Thanks also to my mom, who encouraged me to make the phone call that led to my first job as a country music disc jockey while still in my teen years back in the 1950's. I enjoyed country music as much then as I do now.

Hope you enjoy the time you spend with this book.

Dennis Hazzard

COUNTRY MUSIC

General

1. THE "GRAND OLE OPRY"

1. What was the "Grand Ole Opry" originally called?

2. Who gave the "Grand Ole Opry" its name?

3. Who was the first performer to become a national star through appearances on the "Grand Ole Opry"?

4. What sentimental link has the new "Grand Ole Opry" house with its former home at the Ryman Auditorium?

5. What music giant appeared on the "Grand Ole Opry" but was denied membership?

6. On what radio network was the "Grand Ole Opry" heard from coast to coast?

7. What VIP was part of the premier performance of the "Grand Ole Opry" at its present home?

8. Name the famous "Opry" comedian who was murdered shortly after a Saturday night performance on the "Opry"?

9. This man is the most revered of all present-day "Opry" stars and is the only "Grand Ole Opry" member with his own private dressing room backstage at the "Opry." Name him.

10. During World War II the "Grand Ole Opry" gained widespread prominence through what device?

3

2. COUNTRY STARS AND THEIR NICKNAMES

1. What singer's early nickname was "Mr. Teardrop"?

2. Who is "Whispering Bill"?

3. The "Singing Brakeman" is ————?

4. Name the "Tennessee Plowboy."

5. There's just no stopping "The Killer."

6. The "Possum" is ————.

7. He was known as the "Gentleman."

8. The "Cherokee Cowboy," ————, hails from Texas.

9. His hair is responsible for his nickname, "The Silver Fox." He is ————.

10. ———— was a movie and country music star who carried the nickname "The Arizona Cowboy."

3. NATIONAL BARN DANCES

Barn dances were an important steppingstone to stardom for many country music stars years ago. Name the city and state where these famous country music barn-dance broadcasts originated.

1. WWVA *Jamboree:* ———, ———

2. WLS *Barn Dance:* ———, ———

3. KWKH *Louisiana Hayride:* ———, ———

4. WGN *National Barn Dance:* ———, ———

5. WRVA *Old Dominion Barn Dance:* ———, ———

6. KRLD *Big D Jamboree:* ———, ———

7. KLRA *Barnyard Frolic:* ———, ———

8. WNOX *Tennessee Barn Dance:* ———, ———

9. WLW *Midwestern Hayride:* ———, ———

10. WARL *Radio Ranch:* ———, ———

4. MATCH REAL NAME WITH SINGER'S STAGE NAME

1.	Virginia Hensley	a.	Kitty Wells
2.	Jimmie Loden	b.	Johnny Paycheck
3.	Harold Jenkins	c.	Sonny James
4.	Leonard Slye	d.	Patsy Montana
5.	Rubye Blevins	e.	Patsy Cline
6.	Mary Penick	f.	Roy Rogers
7.	Don Lytle	g.	Conway Twitty
8.	Sarah Ophelia Cannon	h.	Skeeter Davis
9.	Brenda Webb	i.	Crystal Gayle
10.	Muriel Dean	j.	Minnie Pearl

5. NAME THE "COUNTRY COMICS"

1. This much loved country comic is from "Grinder's Switch" and greets her audiences with a big "HOWDEE." Who is she?

2. His banjo playing was equal to his comic ability. He got his nickname from one of his favorite vegetables. Who is this country comic?

3. A record called "I'm My Own Grandpa" was a big seller for this act, which was composed originally of Rollin Sullivan and Dave Hooten. They called themselves "——— and ———".

4. Millions have delighted in hearing this country comic's stories about life in Yazoo City, Mississippi. This comedian is ———.

5. This country comic team made hilarious parodies of popular and country songs. One of their big hits was "That Hound Dog in the Window." Who are they?

6. Name a country comic who is also a painter, musician, and songwriter. He does a hilarious takeoff on "Cinderella" called "Rendercella." ——— stars on *Hee Haw*.

7. Name the country comic whose tag line was "I'm goin' back to the wagon, these shoes are killin' me!" He, too, was a fine musician. His name was ———.

8. Identify this lady who was a hit on Broadway, starred in movies, and had a successful radio show. She also made hit records, primarily in the 1940's. She is———.

9. A Macon, Georgia, disc jockey is credited with playing a taped interview on the radio that launched this country comic's career. He is now featured on *Hee Haw*. Who is he?

10. This man starred on the "Grand Ole Opry" from 1944 until he died in 1958. He travelled in a tent show with his brother prior to joining the "Opry." This country comic performed regularly with Minnie Pearl. Name him.

6. COUNTRY RELATIVES

What is the relationship between each of the following?

1. Dottie and Shelly

2. Lefty and David

3. Buck and Buddy

4. Dolly and Stella

5. La Costa and Tanya

6. Liz and Lynn

7. Ernest and Justin

8. Wilma Lee and Carol

9. Johnny and Rosanne

10. Johnny and Bobby

7. TIME OUT TO UNSCRAMBLE

Unscramble each of the following stars' names. See how many you can get in five minutes. Five of the stars have something in common. What is it?

1. YERJR ELE SIWEL
2. ETATOLR NLYN
3. YJHNNO HACS
4. KNAH WOSN
5. VLSIE YEESRPL
6. IRKYC GACSGS
7. LRCA SNKRIEP
8. NJOH NOREDANS
9. ELRHACI HCRI
10. LGIA SVEIDA

8. REAL FIRST NAMES

Write in the last name of each star.

1. Clyde Julian "Red" ———
2. Laurence Hankins "Hank" ———
3. Frank "Pee Wee" ———
4. Alvis Edgar "Buck" ———
5. Juan Raul Davis "Johnny" ———
6. Clarence Eugene "Hank" ———
7. Woodrow Wilson "Red" ———
8. Otis Dewey "Slim" ———
9. William Orville "Lefty" ———
10. Lloyd "Cowboy" ———

9. MORE . . . MATCH REAL NAME WITH SINGER'S STAGE NAME

1. Calvin Shofner
2. Yvonne Vaughn
3. Eva Sue McKee
4. George Nowlan
5. Baldermar Huerta
6. Bill Browder
7. Ray Ragsdale
8. David Akeman
9. Wynette Pugh
10. William Fries

a. Ray Stevens
b. Stringbean
c. T. G. Sheppard
d. Danny Davis
e. Cal Smith
f. Tammy Wynette
g. Donna Fargo
h. Sue Thompson
i. Freddy Fender
j. C. W. McCall

10. MATCH BANDS WITH THEIR LEADERS

1. "Blue Grass Boys"

2. "The Jones Boys"

3. "Do-Rites"

4. "Coal Miners"

5. "Po Folks"

6. "Smokey Mountain Boys"

7. "Nashville Brass"

8. "Buckaroos"

9. "Statesiders"

10. "Heartbeats"

a. Buck Owens

b. Bill Monroe

c. Danny Davis

d. Freddy Hart

e. Mel Tillis

f. George Jones

g. Barbara Mandrell

h. Loretta Lynn

i. Bill Anderson

j. Roy Acuff

11. COVERS OF COUNTRY HITS

In the 1950's it was nearly impossible for pop music fans to accept country music, so pop artists recorded their versions of country hits. See if you can identify the pop music stars who recorded these country hits.

1. Tex Ritter was responsible for the country hit of "High Noon," while ——— recorded the pop music version.

2. Ray Price's version of "Heartaches by the Number" was released on the same record label that recorded a pop version of the song by ———.

3. Stuart Hamblen's "This Ole House" was made into a pop hit by ———.

4. While Marty Robbins was "Singing the Blues" on the country charts, ——— was making it up the pop charts with his version of the song.

5. "Detour" was a country classic for Elton Britt, and it was the ——— version that was a pop music success.

6. Columbia Records artist———recorded Hank Williams's "Half as Much" for pop music fans.

7. It was Eddy Arnold who turned "Anytime" into a Country music classic. In pop music ——— made it a hit.

8. The Hank Williams hit "Your Cheatin' Heart" was recorded by ——— for pop music lovers.

9. This song was a country hit for Skeets MacDonald, Red Foley, Ray Price, and Slim Willet. It was "Don't Let the Stars Get in Your Eyes," a pop music success for ————.

10. Another Hank Williams hit, "Cold Cold Heart," was a pop music hit for ————.

12. MISCELLANEOUS

1. Name the event held every June in Nashville which attracts thousands of country music lovers from all over the world. They come for a week of live shows featuring some of country's biggest stars and the chance to meet their favorite performers up close.

2. Who was the first black country music star? He was also among the first to record commercially in Nashville.

3. Who's the pretty Australian lass who made it onto the country music charts in the 1970's, although she is primarily a pop/rock singer?

4. What honor was bestowed upon the song "Arizona," recorded by Rex Allen, Jr.?

5. Name the successful songwriter/singer who wrote a hit for Elvis called "In the Ghetto." His self-penned "Hooked on Music" was a 1981 hit.

6. What female singer preceded Dolly Parton as Porter Wagoner's singing partner?

7. It is considered the largest outdoor country music concert and has been held every year since 1977 near a small town in Ohio. What is it called?

8. His first singing partners were his sisters. After solo work he teamed with Helen Cornelius for a string of hits. Who is he?

9. What TV star recorded a duet with Willie Nelson called "Something to Brag About"? She was a star on what show?

10. Name the lady who recorded with her family and is one of country music's pioneers.

13. NETWORK COUNTRY MUSIC TV SHOWS

Network television has almost ignored country music on its prime-time schedule over the years, although some stars and shows have gained exposure on the medium. Identify these network TV country music stars and shows.

1. This star and his show were probably truer to country music's roots than most. The show was seen on ABC from 1969 to 1971, then again as a summer replacement in 1976. Comedian Steve Martin was a regular during the show's 1976 summer run. The star is a legend.

2. NBC featured a country music series in 1974 that was taped at various locations around the country with a different host each week.

3. She and her sisters had a one season show on NBC in 1981–1982. A versatile entertainer, she elected to give up the show because of the physical strain in doing it.

4. For five years, 1955–1960, Red Foley hosted this country music show out of Springfield, Missouri, on ABC. It went through several name changes. Can you remember one?

5. He was probably the first country music star to headline his own network TV show back in 1952. It was only fifteen minutes long, three times a week, and a summer replacement at that. In 1956 he was given

his own weekly half-hour show for one season to showcase his tender ballads.

6. In 1961 NBC presented a country show called *Five Star Jubilee* on Friday nights. Can you name at least one of the five rotating stars of the show?

7. This show had an intermittent run on NBC and ABC from 1951 to 1959, during the summer. It originated from Cincinnati, Ohio. Hardly any of its stars gained national prominence.

8. From 1969 through June 1972, this was a popular weekly show on CBS. John Hartford, Jerry Reed, Larry McNeely, and Dom DeLuise were regulars. The host had a long string of hit records in the late 1960's.

9. Because of a desire to "deruralize" its programming, CBS took this show off its prime-time schedule in 1971, after a two-season run, in spite of its popularity. The producers put the show into syndication, where it has been successful ever since.

10. The "Grandest Lady of Them All" was featured on network television from October 1955 through September 1956. Viewers got a one-hour sampling of the three-hour live radio show.

14. FAMOUS COUNTRY DUETS

Name the famous singing partner and name the year their song was a hit.

1. "Dis-Satisfied": Bill Anderson and ———

2. "Yes, Mr. Peters": Roy Drusky and ———

3. "A Satisfied Mind": Red Foley and ———

4. "Wish I Didn't Have to Miss You": Jack Greene and ———

5. "Morning Comes Too Early": Jim Ed Brown and ———

6. "Suspicious Minds": Waylon Jennings and———

7. "Cup of Tea": Rex Allen, Jr., and ———

8. "There Ain't No Good Chain Gang": Johnny Cash and ———

9. "After Closing Time": David Houston and ———

10. "We Must Have Been Out of Our Minds": George Jones and ———

15. SONGS ABOUT ROSES

The rose has often been a popular subject for country music's songwriters. How many song titles can you identify from the following clues?

1. It was a hit for Mickey Gilley in 1975 and for Eddy Arnold in the 1940's.

2. In addition to roses, what else did Dickey Lee sing about in his 1976 hit?

3. It was a hit for Hank Williams, Jr., in 1972. He was just shy of a dozen roses.

4. Sonny James took this "roses" song to the #1 position on *Billboard*'s charts in 1972. Cold weather was an important part of this song lyric.

5. C. W. McCall's 1977 hit was about giving roses to a certain someone.

6. In 1974 Mickey Gilley took this song about roses to the #1 position on *Billboard*'s charts. He sang about a lot of roses.

7. Lynn Anderson's 1970 "roses" song was a smash hit. No more clues needed on this giant!

8. From 1972 came Marie Osmond's hit record about roses that weren't real.

9. Ray Price combined roses with something else in his 1975 hit record.

10. Tommy Overstreet wanted no roses in his 1972 hit.

16. MORE . . . MATCH BANDS WITH THEIR LEADERS

1. "The Storytellers"   a. Hank Williams

2. "Strangers"   b. Hank Thompson

3. "Texas Troubadors"   c. Bob Wills

4. "Southern Gentlemen"   d. Tom T. Hall

5. "Brazos Valley Boys"   e. Mickey Gilley

6. "Texas Playboys"   f. Merle Haggard

7. "Driftin' Cowboys"   g. Sonny James

8. "Deputies"   h. Ernest Tubb

9. "Cherokee Cowboys"   i. Ray Price

10. "Urban Cowboy Band"   j. Faron Young

17. MORE...NETWORK COUNTRY MUSIC TV SHOWS

1. What country singer had a summer replacement show in 1972, the title for which was taken from one of his hit records? The show was seen on CBS.

2. A successful country music star on Washington, D.C., TV, this singer became a network star on ABC in 1963. Jim Henson of *Muppets* fame created a dog puppet named Rowlf that was a running feature on the show.

3. You're sharp if you remember this early television country music show out of Chicago. It was on Monday nights on ABC from February through November of 1949.

4. Johnny Cash took off for the summer and turned his show over to a pair of singing brothers. The year was 1970 and the network was ABC. Who were the brothers?

5. This show was an early attempt at country music on network television. It originated from Philadelphia and was shown on ABC in 1948 during the summer months.

6. Name the singer who hosted a Saturday night show on ABC during the summer of 1955. His partner was Redd Stewart.

7. This entertainer focused on country music's gospel side and his last name is the same as the sponsor of the popular Thursday night show he hosted.

8. In 1962 this famous couple had a country variety show on ABC on Saturday nights, although it did not run nearly as long as their action-adventure series in the 1950's. He's a "king" and she's his "queen."

9. From May 1948 to May 1950, this show was featured on NBC. It originated from a nightclub in New York City and featured audience-participation games as well as music. You're exceptionally good if you remember the name of this show.

10. Elton Britt hosted this show in 1948 and Boyd Heath took over as host in 1949. Seen on NBC, the show was New York-based and was part of the Saturday night schedule. Partner, if you know this one, you're an expert in country music TV shows for sure!

18. COUNTRY INSTRUMENTALISTS

Match the artists with their instrument.

1. Pee Wee King	a. Fiddle
2. Boots Randolph	b. Banjo
3. Del Wood	c. Trumpet
4. Danny Davis	d. Steel guitar
5. Maybelle Carter	e. Piano
6. Charlie McCoy	f. Accordion
7. Bob Wills	g. Guitar
8. Chet Atkins	h. Saxophone
9. Lloyd Green	i. Harmonica
10. Earl Scruggs	j. Autoharp

19. MATCH THE SINGER WITH HIS—OR HER—HIT SONG

1. "Talk Back Trembling Lips"

   a. Tennessee Ernie Ford

2. "Big Bad John"

   b. Mel McDaniel

3. "I'm Not Lisa"

   c. Wanda Jackson

4. "Louisiana Saturday Night"

   d. Ernie Ashworth

5. "You Are My Sunshine"

   e. Jimmy Dean

6. "Stranger"

   f. Jessi Colter

7. "Sixteen Tons"

   g. Bobby Helms

8. "Gotta Travel On"

   h. Billy Grammer

9. "My Special Angel"

   i. Jimmie Davis

10. "Right or Wrong"

   j. Johnny Duncan

20. ROCK 'N' ROLL AND COUNTRY

Country singers have gone back to the 1950's and 1960's for pop and rock 'n' roll songs to redo "country-style." Here are questions based on this trend.

1. The Big Bopper's version of this song from 1958 was released by Jerry Lee Lewis in 1972. Name the song.

2. Reba McEntire was successful in 1982 with a 1950's hit called "Only You." Who did the original version of the song?

3. In 1959 the Everly Brothers' "('Til) I Kissed You" was a big hit. What country artist recorded the song?

4. Lenny Welch's "Since I Fell for You" (1963) was released by what two country artists?

5. Freddy Fender in 1975 and Sonny James in 1969 both rerecorded a 1956 hit called "Since I Met You Baby." Who recorded the original version?

6. "Funny How Time Slips Away" was a hit for Jimmy Elledge in 1961 on the pop and rock 'n' roll charts. What country artists did versions of the song?

7. A powerful version of a certain 1961 song was done by Timi Yuro. It was also recorded by country's Connie Cato in 1975 and by Elvis. Name the song.

8. Linda Ronstadt sang "It Doesn't Matter Anymore" in 1975. What artist originally recorded the song?

9. This song had a cha-cha beat and was a hit for

Mickey and Sylvia in 1956. Country's Buck Owens and Susan Raye did a successful version of the song in 1975. What's the song?

10. Johnny Mathis must have been startled when he heard Ray Stevens's up-tempo version of this 1959 Mathis ballad. Name the song.

21. SINGING COWBOYS

1. This entertainer was important in radio, records, and movies. He was in more than fifty western films and even dabbled in politics. His screen horse's name was "White Flash." Name him.

2. Name the singing cowboy who made over one hundred films, starred on radio and television, and made records. The horse he rode was nearly as popular as the "King of the Cowboys."

3. Gene Autry gave this star a helping hand when he made him a part of his band. He later performed with his own group. He teamed with Margaret Whiting for several hit records. Who is this singing cowboy?

4. He was one of the screen's earliest singing cowboys throughout the 1930's and 1940's. He cowrote Gene Autry's theme, "Back in the Saddle Again." At one time he was a singing sidekick to Tim Holt. Name him.

5. He made his first film with Tex Ritter in the late 1930's and continued making them into the 1950's. His records were well received and his giant hit was "Smoke, Smoke, Smoke." Who is he?

6. "The Arizona Cowboy" was featured in thirty-two Republic films from 1950 to 1957. He had previously appeared on radio and made hit records in the 1950's. His son has become a major country music star. Who is he?

7. Name the country music giant who in later life has built an empire that includes major league baseball ownership and a chain of radio and television stations. This singing cowboy starred in over one hundred musical westerns and had a successful series on radio and television. He rode a horse named "Champion." Identify him.

8. He was known for a time as the "King of Western Swing" and appeared in many western films in the 1930's and 1940's. He had one of the biggest bands in country music, sometimes numbering about two dozen musicians. His biggest hit was in 1945 with "Shame on You." Who is he?

9. He was the first cowboy to sing on film. He was also the first to use a western song as a film title and introduced Gene Autry in films in a 1934 film called *Santa Fe*. He was also a stunt man.

10. Name another Gene Autry discovery who appeared with Autry on radio and in films. He was also a songwriter who composed more than four hundred songs during his career. One of his big hits was "Divorce Me C.O.D." Name him.

22. ANOTHER ROUND OF MATCH THE SINGER WITH THE HIT SONG

1. "You and Me Against the World"

   a. Sammi Smith

2. "Let's Think About Livin' "

   b. T. G. Sheppard

3. "Candy Kisses"

   c. Kenny Price

4. "A Fallen Star"

   d. Bobby Lord

5. "Go Cat Go"

   e. George Morgan

6. "The Sheriff of Boone County"

   f. Jimmy C. Newman

7. "Girl on the Billboard"

   g. Bob Luman

8. "You Lay So Easy on My Mind"

   h. Del Reeves

9. "Last Cheater's Waltz"

   i. Bobby G. Rice

10. "Help Me Make it Through the Night"

   j. Norma Jean

23. UNSCRAMBLE TIME

Unscramble the names of these country artists. Give yourself five minutes. When you've finished, determine what six of the singers share in a common sports interest.

1. LILB NOSDERAN

2. YANAT RECKTU

3. OYR FUCAF

4. OBB MALUN

5. YCLRHEA IPEDR

6. EHCRILA INADELS

7. MJI SEVERE

8. NLEG LELBAMCP

9. CKBU NSOWE

10. YACNOW TTWTIY

24. MORE ROCK 'N' ROLL AND COUNTRY

Match the original with the country artist who recorded the song.

1. "Secret Love," Doris
   Day   a. Tom T. Hall

2. "What in the World's
   Come Over You,"
   Jack Scott   b. Linda Ronstadt

3. "When Will I Be
   Loved," Everly
   Brothers   c. Billy "Crash" Craddock

4. "Stand By Me," Ben
   E. King   d. David Rogers

5. "It's All in the Game,"
   Tommy Edwards   e. Marie Osmond

6. "Ruby Baby," Dion   f. Freddy Fender

7. "Need You," Donnie
   Owens   g. Jerry Lee Lewis

8. "Paper Roses," Anita
   Bryant   h. Sonny James

9. "I'm Leavin' It All Up
   to You," Dale
   and Grace   i. Mickey Gilley

10. "Lonely Weekends,"
    Charlie Rich   j. Freddy Fender

25. TV AND MOVIE THEMES ... "COUNTRY STYLE"

1. Merle Haggard wrote and sang the theme song for a TV show featuring Claude Akins and Frank Converse. Name the show.

2. What was the Johnny Paycheck song that became the basis for a 1981 movie?

3. "The Ballad of Johnny Yuma" by Johnny Cash was a hit record and the theme for what TV series? Name the star of the series, too.

4. Who sang the theme song for the Gary Cooper film *High Noon?*

5. The theme for *Every Which Way but Loose,* a Clint Eastwood film, was sung by what country star?

6. Name the TV series for which Waylon Jennings created and sang the theme song.

7. Marty Robbins recorded the title song for a western starring Gary Cooper. What was the film?

8. The Clampett family on the *Beverly Hillbillies* TV series was introduced by what song and artists?

9. Name the country star who wrote and recorded the theme for her first film. Also name the film.

10. Name another TV theme song recorded by the same people who did the *Beverly Hillbillies* theme.

26. TRUCK DRIVIN' SINGERS AND SONGS

1. "I Love My Truck" was a 1981 hit for ———.

2. What kind of truck was sung about by John Anderson in his 1981 hit?

3. What was Joe Stampley's big truckin' song from 1975?

4. In 1976 Red Sovine's song about a child and a trucker was a giant hit. Name the song.

5. Name the truckin' song that was a hit for C. W. McCall in 1975 and was later used as the basis for a movie.

6. "Truck Drivin' Son of a Gun" was recorded by ———.

7. What female singer recorded a truck drivin' song called, "Truck Drivin' Woman"? It was out in 1968, but wasn't a big hit.

8. "Truck Drivin' Man" was a 1964 hit for ———?

9. Dave Dudley had a hit in 1963, probably the earliest top-ten truckin' song. What was it?

10. The 1971 hit "I'm a Truck" was recorded by ———.

27. MATCH 'EM UP, PARTNER!

Match the star with the hit record. Then see if you can determine what common occupation each held before reaching stardom.

1.	John Conlee	a.	"Still"
2.	Tennessee Ernie Ford	b.	"Gone"
3.	Bill Anderson	c.	"I Ain't Living Long Like This"
4.	Ferlin Husky	d.	"Rose Colored Glasses"
5.	Johnny Duncan	e.	"He'll Have to Go"
6.	Charlie Walker	f.	"Sixteen Tons"
7.	Jim Reeves	g.	"Thinking of a Rendez-vous"
8.	Willie Nelson	h.	"The Year That Clayton Delaney Died"
9.	Tom T. Hall	i.	"Pick Me Up on Your Way Down"
10.	Waylon Jennings	j.	"Blue Eyes Crying in the Rain"

28. MORE MATCH THE SINGER WITH THE HIT SONG

1. "Blind Man in the Bleachers"

   a. Porter Wagoner

2. "Lone Star Beer and Bob Wills Music"

   b. Jerry Wallace

3. "It's Such A Pretty World Today"

   c. Leroy van Dyke

4. "Walk on By"

   d. Dottie West

5. "Misery Loves Company"

   e. Red Steagall

6. "Charlie's Shoes"

   f. Wynn Stewart

7. "If You Leave Me To-night I'll Cry"

   g. Kenny Starr

8. "Here Comes My Baby"

   h. Mac Wiseman

9. "Indian Love Call"

   i. Billy Walker

10. "Jimmy Brown, the Newsboy"

   j. Slim Whitman

29. FROM THE SIDELINES TO STARDOM

Established country stars have given a frequent helping hand to aspiring talent. Match the singer with the act he or she performed with in the early stages of his career.

1. Jack Greene and Cal Smith

2. Johnny Rodriguez

3. Gary Stewart

4. Flatt and Scruggs

5. Eddy Arnold

6. Dave Rowland (before "Sugar")

7. Gene Watson

8. Waylon Jennings

9. Johnny Paycheck

10. Wanda Jackson

a. Faron Young's "Deputies"

b. "The Imperials" and "The Four Guys"

c. Pee Wee King's "Golden West Cowboys"

d. Charley Pride's "Pridesmen"

e. Ernest Tubb's "Troubadors"

f. Wilburn Brothers

g. Hank Thompson's "Brazos Valley Boys"

h. Tom T. Hall's "Storytellers"

i. Buddy Holly's "Crickets"

j. Bill Monroe's "Blue Grass Boys"

30. COUNTRY MUSIC DATES

Name the year in which the following country-music-related events occurred.

1. Tragic plane crash takes the life of Johnny Horton.

2. The name of the WSM *Barn Dance* is changed to the "Grand Ole Opry."

3. The Carter family is recorded by Ralph Peer in Bristol, Tennessee.

4. On the way to a show in Canton, Ohio, the legendary Hank Williams dies.

5. The first commercial recording session held in Nashville.

6. Patsy Cline, Hawkshaw Hawkins, and Cowboy Copas die in an air disaster at Camden, Tennessee.

7. The dedication and first performance at the new Grand Ole Opry House.

8. Jim Reeves dies with his manager just outside Nashville in a single-engine plane crash.

9. Tuberculosis takes the life of the "Singing Brakeman," Jimmie Rodgers.

10. The "King of Country Music," Roy Acuff, is born in Maynardsville, Tennessee.

31. COUNTRY NOVELTY SONGS AND ARTISTS

1. Name the record by Ray Stevens that related to a wild time by a large gathering of people.

2. Who did the takeoff of Patti Page's "How Much Is That Doggie in the Window"? What was their title?

3. What was Ferlin Husky's comic alter ego?

4. Name the Ray Stevens hit that contained a warning to "Ethel" to "look out."

5. What is comic Ben Colder's real name?

6. Who was "Shirley's" singing partner on the 1976 novelty record?

7. What Faron Young song did Ben Colder spoof in 1963?

8. On what Homer and Jethro song did June Carter sing in 1949?

9. David Houston probably split his sides laughing at Ben Colder's take-off of what Houston hit?

10. In 1959 Homer and Jethro spoofed the biggest hit of that year, a record by the late Johnny Horton. What was their version called?

32. MORE ROCK 'N' ROLL AND COUNTRY

Match the country artist and song to the original artist who recorded the song.

1. "That'll Be the Day," Linda Ronstadt

   a. Johnny Ray

2. "True Love Ways," Mickey Gilley

   b. Gene Pitney

3. "Cry," Lynn Anderson

   c. James Ray

4. "Slippin' and Slidin,' " Billy "Crash" Craddock

   d. Connie Francis

5. "Only Love Can Break A Heart," Sonny James

   e. Buddy Holly and the Crickets

6. "If You Got to Make a Fool of Somebody," Dickey Lee

   f. Ames Brothers

7. "Pledging My Love," Elvis

   g. Clyde McPhatter

8. "My Heart Has A Mind of Its Own," Susan Raye and Debby Boone

   h. Peter and Gordon

9. "It Only Hurts for A Little While," Margo Smith

   i. Roy Hamilton

10. "A Lover's Question," Jacky Ward

    j. Little Richard

33. COUNTRY MUSIC ASSOCIATION AWARDS

1. When are the Country Music Association Awards presented and what is significant about that month?

2. What company is associated with sponsorship of the annual telecast?

3. Who was the first female singer to win the "Entertainer of the Year" award?

4. What artist has won the "Entertainer of the Year" award more than once?

5. Name the other female to win the "Entertainer of the Year" award.

6. Ben Colder, Don Bowman, Archie Campbell, and Roy Clark each won a CMA award in which category that has since been discontinued?

7. Charley Pride, Ronnie Milsap, and George Jones have something in common with CMA awards. What is it?

8. A new category was introduced in 1981 called the "Horizon Award." Who was its first recipient?

9. What artist has won the "Instrumentalist of the Year" award more than any other—Chet Atkins, Charlie McCoy, or Roy Clark?

10. What vocal duo has won the award for "Best of the Year" more than any other?

34. MORE COUNTRY MUSIC ASSOCI-
ATION AWARDS

1. What group has won the "Vocal Group of the Year" award more than any other?

2. In 1976 and again in 1980 the "Vocal Duo" award went to other than a male/female duet. Can you name the male duets that won in those years?

3. From 1969 through 1974 the "Instrumental Group or Band of the Year" award was won by what band or group?

4. A mother and daughter have both won the same award, but not at the same time. Can you name them and the award they won?

5. Two songs have won for two consecutive years each in the "Song of the Year" category. Name them.

6. Two songs recorded by Kenny Rogers have won as "Song of the Year." Name them.

7. What artist has won more awards in the "Album of the Year" category than any other?

8. In 1965 one artist made a clean sweep in five categories. Who was it?

9. What singer has received "Male Vocalist of the Year" more times than any other?

10. Only one artist has won the coveted "Female Vocalist of the Year" award three years in a row. Name her.

35. MORE MATCH THE SINGER WITH THE HIT SONG

1. "Country Bumpkin"

2. "Let Me Be the One"

3. "Ode to Billie Joe"

4. "Teddy Bear Song"

5. "Storms Never Last"

6. "May the Bird of Paradise Fly Up Your Nose"

7. "Would You Lay With Me"

8. "Don't Let Me Cross Over"

9. "LA International Airport"

10. "Gonna Find Me a Bluebird"

a. Carl and June Butler

b. Barbara Fairchild

c. "Little" Jimmy Dickens

d. Marvin Rainwater

e. Bobbie Gentry

f. Cal Smith

g. Dottsy

h. Hank Locklin

i. David Allan Coe

j. Susan Raye

43

36. FAMOUS COUNTRY BROTHERS

Give the last names of these country music brother acts.

1. Sam and Kirk

2. Jim and Jesse

3. Harold and Don

4. Larry, Steve, and Rudy

5. Bill and Charlie

6. Dave and Howard

7. Tompall, Chuck, and Jim

8. Teddy and Doyle

9. Ira and Charlie

10. Bill and Cliff

37. ROCK 'N' ROLL AND COUNTRY CONTINUED

1. Jerry Lee Lewis had a 1957 hit with "Great Balls of Fire." What country artist brought it back in 1979?

2. Sonny James recorded a country version of "Born to Be With You" in 1971. What 1950's group did the song first?

3. "Peanut Butter," a novelty song, was a pop/rock hit for the Marathons. Who did the country version?

4. Several early 1950's versions of "If I Give My Heart to You" were on the pop charts. Who in country music recorded the song in 1979?

5. A Roy Hamilton hit from 1961, "You Can Have Her," was recorded by what twosome for country fans?

6. Name the song popularized by Fats Domino in the 1950's and given a country treatment by Hank Williams, Jr., in 1971.

7. A Jack Scott 1960 hit called "Burning Bridges" was rerecorded by what country artist in 1966?

8. What rock 'n' roll singer did "It's Just A Matter of Time," rerecorded by country singer Sonny James in 1970?

9. Name the country duo that recorded in 1970 the Everly Brothers hit from 1959 called "All I Have to Do Is Dream."

10. The song "Only the Lonely," a 1960 hit for Roy Orbison, was a country hit for what artist?

38. SINGING HUSBANDS AND WIVES

1. She's Barbara's sister, and his first initials are those of a popular soft drink.

2. He's the "Man in Black" and she's the lady who helped "turn him around."

3. Both were considered "outlaws" in the early 1970's.

4. Although privately they can't make it together, on record they are "dynamite."

5. She's the "Queen" and he is her "King."

6. "The Bull and the Beaver" was a hit for them in 1978.

7. The year 1959 was a good one for this couple whose "There's a Big Wheel" was one of their hits that year.

8. A song about a camel named "Humphrey" is one of this couple's hits.

9. She divorced Buck Owens and married another country star. He's been mentioned on the page previously.

10. He's a "Smith" and she's remembered as a "Hill" on stage. They're the only couple listed on this page never to have a hit record together.

39. MISCELLANEOUS TRIVIA

1. What former pop singer turned country/gospel singer became a member of the Grand Ole Opry in 1982?

2. Besides the CMA Awards Show, name two other major country music awards given on television yearly.

3. Songwriter-singer Ed Bruce was a featured player on what TV series?

4. What short-lived TV series featured Jerry Reed as a character named Trace Mayne?

5. What artist has a band named the Hurricanes?

6. Name the singer whose style is considered "southern rock." He performed at President Carter's Inaugural Ball and has won four CMA awards, including one for "Single of the Year" in 1979.

7. From what state do more country music singers come than any other?

8. Name the singer who won a CMA award for "Entertainer of the Year" the same year he won for "Song of the Year" for a song he wrote called "Back Home Again."

9. What do Charlie Douglas, Lee Arnold, Hairl Hensley, Billy Cole, and Lee Shannon have in common?

10. Singer Freddy Weller was once a member of what 1960's rock group?

40. SONGS WITH A CITY TITLE

Match the song with the artist.

1. "Big in Vegas"	a. Mel Tillis
2. "Streets of Baltimore"	b. Lefty Frizzell
3. "Sidewalks of Chicago"	c. Don Gibson
4. "Send Me Down to Tucson"	d. Roger Miller
5. "Saginaw, Michigan"	e. Buck Owens
6. "Galveston"	f. Merle Haggard
7. "If You Ever Get to Houston (Look Me Down)"	g. Webb Pierce
8. "Kansas City Star"	h. Jerry Lee Lewis
9. "Tupelo County Jail"	i. Glen Campbell
10. "What's Made Milwaukee Famous"	j. Bobby Bare

41. A COUNTRY CHRISTMAS

1. Although it didn't make the country charts, Brenda Lee's ———— has been a Christmas favorite for years.

2. Name the Gene Autry Christmas hit that was all about an animal that helped Santa.

3. The song "C-H-R-I-S-T-M-A-S" was a hit for what country artist in 1949?

4. Who popularized the Christmas song "Frosty the Snowman"?

5. Bobby Helms's Christmas hit, ————, did not make the country charts, but every country fan knows and loves it.

6. What artist had a seasonal hit with "Blue Christmas" in 1949?

7. What is another giant Christmas hit by Gene Autry that has been a standard for many years?

8. Although it was never on the charts, the Christmas song "Santa Claus Is Back in Town" was recorded by what artist and has been a Christmas staple ever since.

9. "White Christmas," by ————, was a Christmas entry in 1949.

10. "Will Santa Come to Shanty Town?" was a hit for what country artist?

42. SONGS WITH A CITY TITLE, PART TWO

1. "By the Time I Get to Phoenix"

   a. Bobby Bare

2. "Santa Barbara"

   b. Waylon Jennings and Willie

3. "Tulsa Time"

   c. Marty Robbins

4. "Pittsburgh Stealers"

   d. Charley Pride

5. "Detroit City"

   e. Ronnie Milsap

6. "Cincinnati, Ohio"

   f. Kendalls

7. "El Paso"

   g. George Hamilton IV

8. "Is Anyone Goin' to San Antone"

   h. Connie Smith

9. "Fort Worth, Dallas or Houston"

   i. Don Williams

10. "Luckenbach, Texas"

    j. Glen Campbell

43. ANSWER SONGS

Answer songs are those that follow up the original hit with a reply. How many of the following questions can you answer correctly?

1. What was the answer song to Hank Thompson's "Wild Side of Life," and who recorded it?

2. David Houston's "Almost Persuaded" was answered by a comic version by what country artist?

3. It was Roger Miller's "King of the Road" answered by Jody Miller's ———.

4. The Jim Reeves hit "He'll Have to Go" was answered by Jeanne Black's ———.

5. An answer to "Teddy Bear" was recorded by Diana Williams and was called ———.

6. "Wolverton Mountain" by Claude King was answered by Jo Anne Campbell's ———.

7. Ben Colder provided a funny answer to what Faron Young hit?

8. Skeeter Davis's "I Can't Help You I'm Falling Too" was an answer to "Please Help Me I'm Falling" by ———.

9. Sunday Sharpe was successful with an answer song called "I'm Having Your Baby." Who recorded the original pop song "You're Having My Baby"?

10. Ben Colder provided an answer of sorts to what giant hit by Jeannie C. Riley?

44. NASHVILLE AND TENNESSEE SONGS

Match the song with the singer.

1. "Tennessee River"   a. Osborne Brothers

2. "Tennessee Rose"   b. Ray Stevens

3. "Tennessee Birdwalk"   c. Patti Page

4. "Nashville"   d. Red Foley

5. "Tennessee Waltz"*   e. Alabama

6. "Sunday Down in   f. Jack Blanchard and
   Tennessee"   Misty Morgan

7. "Tennessee Saturday
   Night"   g. Emmylou Harris

8. "Tennessee Stud"   h. Eddy Arnold

9. "Rocky Top"*   i. Red Foley

*What do "Tennessee Waltz" and "Rocky Top" have in common?

45. MATCH THE NICKNAME WITH THE STAR

1. "Bocephus"
2. "Rabbit"
3. "The Alabama Wild Man"
4. "The Singing Ranger"
5. "The Ragin' Cajun"
6. "The Bear"
7. "The Chocolate Cowboy"
8. "Mr. Guitar"
9. "Little Miss Dynamite"
10. "Queen of Country Music"

a. Bobby Bare
b. Chet Atkins
c. O. B. McClinton
d. Brenda Lee
e. Hank Williams, Jr.
f. Roy Acuff
g. Kitty Wells
h. Hank Snow
i. Jerry Reed
j. Doug Kershaw

46. ANOTHER ROUND OF ROCK 'N' ROLL AND COUNTRY

1. A group called The Association recorded this hit song in 1967. Who recorded the country version of "Never My Love"?

2. Jacky Ward's "Rhythm of the Rain" from 1978 was recorded by what pop/rock group in 1963?

3. Name the song recorded by the Drifters in 1960 that Jerry Lee Lewis rerecorded in 1978 and Emmylou Harris rerecorded in 1979.

4. Elvis's "Unchained Melody" hit the top ten on the country charts in 1978. What pop artist did the song in the early 1950's?

5. Several Everly Brothers hits have been rerecorded by country artists. Which Everlys hit did Anne Murray release in 1978?

6. The Paris Sisters were successful in 1961 with a song called "I Love How You Love Me." What country artist did the song in 1979?

7. Rex Allen, Jr., and Andy Williams both recorded this song; Williams in 1959, Allen in 1977. Name the song.

8. The beat was altered, but "Heartbreak Hotel," an Elvis classic from 1956, was a smash hit for what two singers in 1979?

9. An old Chuck Berry tune also recorded by Johnny Rivers was a top-ten country hit for George Jones and Johnny Paycheck in 1978. Name the song.

10. In the early 1950's Kitty Kallen's version of "Little Things Mean a Lot" was a big pop music hit. What country artist did this song?

47. FORMER OCCUPATIONS MATCH

1. John Conlee
2. Anne Murray
3. Sylvia
4. Kris Kristofferson
5. George Jones
6. Emmylou Harris
7. Royce Kendall
8. Roger Miller
9. Mickey Gilley
10. Moe Bandy

a. Rodeo clown
b. Janitor
c. Housepainter
d. Waitress
e. Mortician
f. Teacher
g. Secretary
h. Barber
i. Bellhop
j. Construction worker

48. SONGS WITH A CITY TITLE, PART THREE

1. "San Antonio Stroll"

2. "Battle of New Orleans"

3. "Abilene"

4. "Wichita Lineman"

5. "Jackson"

6. "Kansas City Song"

7. "How I Got to Memphis"

8. "Birmingham Bounce"

9. "Baltimore"

10. "Okie from Muskogee"

a. Johnny Cash and June Carter Cash

b. Buck Owens

c. Red Foley

d. Sonny James

e. George Hamilton IV

f. Tanya Tucker

g. Johnny Horton

h. Merle Haggard

i. Glen Campbell

j. Bobby Bare

49. COUNTRY POLITICS AND BOOKS

1. Merle Haggard's autobiography is titled ———.

2. Roy Acuff ran for what office, but was defeated?

3. ——— is the name of Jeannie C. Riley's autobiography.

4. What country singer was elected governor of Louisiana?

5. Tammy Wynette's autobiography has the same name as one of her hit records. Name the song.

6. Tex Ritter aspired to a career in politics and ran unsuccessfully for what office?

7. Johnny Cash's autobiography is called ———.

8. In the 1960's Hank Locklin was elected to what office in his hometown of McLellan, Florida?

9. What country star's autobiography is called *Living Proof*?

10. What country singer ran for president in 1952 on the Prohibition party ticket?

50. MISCELLANEOUS

1. What singer has a road in Hendersonville, Tennessee, named after him?

2. Who claims he put sex into country music?

3. The first country artist to feature an electric guitar in his act is generally thought to be ————.

4. What group is named for a city in Tennessee?

5. Lester "Roadhog" Moran is really ————.

6. Who played Mrs. Johnson in the TV series based on the song "Harper Valley P.T.A."?

7. What pioneer country singers recorded their first songs the same week in 1927?

8. What artist is associated with Coca-Cola, and why?

9. Jim Owen is renowned for his one-man performances as what legendary country singer?

10. Who hosted *Pop Goes the Country*, a syndicated TV show, before Tom T. Hall, the present host?

COUNTRY
PERSONALITIES

51. MEL TILLIS

1. What's Mel's home state?

2. What female singer did Mel record duets with during his years on MGM records?

3. What kind of revival did Mel sing about in 1976?

4. Name the soda pop Mel used in the title of one of his hit songs.

5. What kind of healer did Mel sing about in 1977?

6. Mel is a frequent guest of what television talk show host?

7. Whose angel did Mel sing about in his hit record?

8. Mel appeared on what TV show in a comedy role?

9. What CMA award did Mel win in 1976?

10. What artist recorded more than thirty songs written by Mel during the mid 1950's and early 1960's?

52. BILL ANDERSON

1. Bill claims what state as his home state?

2. Name the syndicated TV show Bill has hosted in the early 1980's out of Nashville.

3. In the late 1970's Bill changed the name of his band from what to what?

4. What is the name of the TV soap opera Bill is sometimes featured in?

5. Bill wrote a song recorded by Ray Price that helped establish him as a songwriter. Name the song.

6. In addition to being a disc jockey Bill also spent time working in another medium. Identify it.

7. Complete this Bill Anderson song title: "Bright Lights and ————."

8. What was the score between the liars and believers in Bill's hit song?

9. What 1963 Bill Anderson record was both a pop hit and a country hit?

10. What kind of drops did Bill sing about in his 1966 hit record?

53. JOHNNY CASH

1. Name the two musicians who recorded and performed with Johnny as the Tennessee Two during the 1950's.

2. June Carter Cash and Johnny recorded a Grammy-award-winning duet in 1967 about a town. Name the town.

3. What kind of queen did Johnny sing about in 1958?

4. Johnny worked at what job after his discharge from the U.S. Air Force?

5. Is there such a car as the one described in the Cash song, "One Piece at a Time"?

6. Name two subjects Johnny has sung about on his albums.

7. The question in a Johnny Cash song was "How High's the Water, Mama." What was the answer?

8. What prison did Johnny sing about and eventually record one of his albums in?

9. Name the film Johnny starred in with Kirk Douglas in 1970.

10. What influence has Dr. Nat Winston had in Johnny's life?

54. KENNY ROGERS

1. What two Kenny Rogers songs were the basis for TV films?

2. Of what singing group was Kenny a member before being associated with the First Edition?

3. Kenny is an accomplished ———.

4. What song written by Mel Tillis was a hit for Kenny when he was with the First Edition?

5. In addition to recording duets with Dottie West, what other female singer had a hit record with Kenny?

6. Kenny also has talents as a ———.

7. What Kenny Rogers hit won a CMA "Single of the Year" award in 1977?

8. Name the song penned by pop songwriter/singer Lionel Richie that was a giant hit for Kenny in 1981.

9. Kenny's wife Marianne has been featured in what syndicated TV show?

10. What Sonny and Cher song did Kenny and Dottie West make a country music hit in the late 1970's?

55. ERNEST TUBB

1. What pop music group of the 1940's recorded with Ernest?

2. Ernest has a unique way of thanking his fans after singing a song. How does he do this?

3. Where did Ernest serve as headliner for a country music show that was the first of its kind in the facility?

4. Ernest has a famous business in Nashville. What kind of business is it?

5. What star did Ernest introduce on the "Grand Ole Opry" for the first time?

6. Name the country artist who greatly influenced Ernest.

7. Ernest has starred on television, records, and radio. What other area has featured his talents?

8. What coveted honor was bestowed upon Ernest by the CMA?

9. Name the song Ernest wrote that was a hit for him in the 1940's and has since become his theme song.

10. What was the song Ernest recorded during the Korean War that became one of his biggest hits?

56. EDDY ARNOLD

1. Eddy was born in the state of ————.

2. What CMA award was Eddy the first to receive?

3. One of Eddy's hits became his theme song. What is it?

4. Name the Arnold hit that featured him yodeling.

5. For what record company has Eddy recorded since the 1940's?

6. Where did Eddy say he would hold you in his 1948 hit record?

7. In what area has Eddy maintained an interest because of his early background?

8. What product did Eddy advertise on television commercials?

9. What kind of "baby" did Eddy sing about in 1948?

10. What uniqueness has Eddy's career in records had?

57. RONNIE MILSAP

1. What is Ronnie's home state?

2. What is Ronnie's great interest, aside from his music and family?

3. In 1977 the CMA honored Ronnie with what coveted award?

4. Name the 1960's song Ronnie rerecorded in 1982.

5. Ronnie had intentions of becoming a ——— before the music bug hit him.

6. What was Ronnie's first release for RCA records?

7. Ronnie recorded an album of songs previously done by what artist?

8. What kind of dream problems did Ronnie have in one of his hit songs?

9. In 1977 two Milsap songs hit the top of the charts. One was "It Was Almost Like a Song." Can you name the other one?

10. One of Ronnie's album titles poked fun at his blindness. What was it called?

58. MARTY ROBBINS

1. Name Marty's home state.

2. One city in Texas was the source of two hit songs by Marty. Name the city.

3. What was the name of the syndicated TV show Marty once hosted?

4. Marty earned professional respect for his involvement in what sport?

5. Why did Marty like to appear on the last segment of the "Grand Ole Opry" broadcasts?

6. Marty was probably the greatest champion of what special type of music?

7. Besides being an excellent singer, Marty was also equally talented as a ————.

8. During the 1950's Marty was a cross-over artist, with many of his records accepted by both country fans and teenage pop music fans. Can you name Marty's first big cross-over hit?

9. What significance have these titles? *The Gun and the Gavel, The Badge of Marshall Brennan,* and *Buffalo Gun.*

10. Marty had the distinction of being the last performer on what show?

59. STATLER BROTHERS

1. Home state of the Statler Brothers is ————.

2. The group got their name from what source?

3. A 1965 hit for the group started them on the way to the top. The song was a pop and country hit called ————.

4. What movie cowboy did the Statlers immortalize on one of their hit records?

5. Nostalgia has been the theme of many Statler recordings. What high school class did they sing about in 1973?

6. The Statlers formerly used what name for their group?

7. In 1979 the Statlers gave musical advice on how to be a what?

8. The Statlers produced an album that was a takeoff of what type of radio show?

9. What holiday is very special to the Statler Brothers, and why?

10. With what country artist did the Statlers tour at one time?

60. KITTY WELLS

1. Kitty's home state is Tennessee, and she was born in the city of ————.

2. With what radio show was Kitty associated in the early days of her career?

3. Kitty's husband is singer ————.

4. Kitty achieved what distinction on the country music charts?

5. In 1976 Kitty received the CMA's highest honor. What was it?

6. What do Roy Drusky, Red Foley, and Webb Pierce have in common with regard to Kitty?

7. Whose guitar did Kitty sing about in 1959?

8. What was Kitty's biggest 1961 hit?

9. How many ways were there to love you according to Kitty's 1957 record?

10. What Wells classic did Emmylou Harris rerecord in the early 1980's?

61. DONNA FARGO

1. Name Donna's home state.

2. What subject did Donna teach?

3. Donna's first record went to #1 on *Billboard*'s charts. What was it?

4. Donna's next two hits were also *Billboard* chart toppers. What were they?

5. In 1972 her first release received an honor from the CMA. What was it?

6. Besides being a fine vocalist Donna is also quite a ————.

7. What song with a patriotic theme was a Donna Fargo hit in 1974?

8. What early 1950's song did Donna rerecord in 1977?

9. What is the name of Donna's band?

10. Donna's positive attitude toward life was expressed in a 1974 hit called ————.

62. TOM T. HALL

1. Tom was born in the state of ————.

2. Tom wrote one of country music's biggest hits, record-ed by Jeannie C. Riley. What is it?

3. What song does Tom almost always include in his concerts that was not one of his hit records?

4. Name the object that Tom saluted in a 1970 hit record.

5. A 1971 Tom T. Hall hit was based on an actual per-son in Tom's life who died before achieving fame. What was the song?

6. What was it Tom liked in a 1975 record?

7. Tom wrote and sang about old dogs and children in a 1972 record. What other subject was mentioned in the song?

8. What bluegrass favorite did Tom record in 1976?

9. What became president in Tom's 1972 hit?

10. Complete these Tom T. Hall song titles:
    "I ———"
    "Ravishing ———"
    "——— Is"

63. BARBARA MANDRELL

1. Barbara is from the state of ———.

2. How did Barbara meet her husband, Ken Dudney?

3. Name the instruments Barbara generally plays on her show.

4. On what network was Barbara featured in her own weekly variety show with her sisters until the physical strain became too much for Barbara and she discontinued it?

5. What other CMA award has Barbara won twice besides "Entertainer of the Year"?

6. Barbara was the first country artist to appear in what country?

7. The first chart-topping hit for Barbara was in 1978 and was about sleeping arrangements. What was the song?

8. From what person has Barbara received important career advice?

9. Name Barbara's talented sisters.

10. Complete these Mandrell song titles:
    "The Best ——— ———"
    "Fooled ——— ——— ———"
    "——— ——— Not to Each Other"

64. WILLIE NELSON

1. Willie was born in the state of ———.

2. Willie once played bass for ———.

3. What country superstar was given a helping hand by Willie?

4. What artists recorded these songs penned by Nelson? "Crazy," "Hello Walls," and "Night Life"

5. Besides being a songwriter and singer, what other entertainment domain has Willie successfully entered?

6. Willie is considered to be the greatest reflection of what country music image?

7. What legendary event is Willie noted for staging?

8. An album called "Wanted—The Outlaws" won a CMA "Album of the Year" award in 1976. Name the artists who are featured on the album with Willie.

9. Name the Elvis hit that Willie recorded with Leon Russell in 1979.

10. Name the artist Willie paid tribute to in an album. What was the name of the album?

65. WHO AM I?

1. I was born in Louisiana.

2. Webb Pierce took me on the road as a featured vocalist.

3. I won an Army talent show and toured the world entertaining troops.

4. In the 1950's I was a member of the "Grand Ole Opry."

5. I appeared in a 1958 movie called *Country Music Holiday* with Ferlin Husky.

6. In the 1960's I did extensive touring of countries such as Germany, France, Mexico, and England.

7. I was the owner of the *Music City News* for some years.

8. Other business interests of mine have included a race track, booking agency, music publishing firm, and an office building.

9. Some of my 1950's hits are: "If You Ain't Lovin'," "Live Fast Love Hard and Die Young," "I've Got Five Dollars," and "Country Girl."

10. My 1960's hits include "Hello Walls," "The Yellow Bandana," and "Wine Me Up."

66. DON WILLIAMS

1. Don was born in the state of ————.

2. Don was a member of what singing group early in his career?

3. In what movie did Don appear with Burt Reynolds?

4. What Williams song was rerecorded by Waylon Jennings?

5. What CMA award did Don win in 1978?

6. Why is Don referred to by fellow artists and songwriters as a "doctor"?

7. What is Don's typical stage attire?

8. What was Don's first big hit?

9. What Williams song was voted an all-time favorite country record in England?

10. Complete these Williams song titles:
    "Listen ———— ———— ————"
    "Till the ———— ———— ———— ————"
    "Tulsa ————"

67. RAY PRICE

1. Ray's another country star from the state of ———.

2. In college Ray's interests were primarily in ———.

3. A radio broadcast out of Dallas, portions of which were carried on CBS, established Ray on a national level. What was the show?

4. Ray used members of what band to form his Cherokee Cowboys band?

5. What singer-songwriter besides Willie Nelson worked with Ray in his band?

6. What daring "new sound" did Ray add to a 1956 hit of his called "Make the World Go Away"?

7. Name the Ray Price album which won "Best Album of the Year" in 1971 from the CMA.

8. Ray's first #1 hit on the *Billboard* charts was ———.

9. What instrument did Ray's band reportedly become the first to use on the stage of the "Grand Ole Opry"?

10. Complete these Ray Price song titles:
    "My Shoes ——— ——— ——— ——— ———"
    "Heartaches ——— ——— ———"

68. PATSY CLINE

1. Patsy was born in the state of ———.

2. Patsy's big break came as a result of winning what national talent show on television?

3. What recording of hers was released in 1957 and became a hit on both the country and pop charts?

4. In what year was Patsy posthumously voted into the "Country Music Hall of Fame"?

5. Which of Patsy's hit records was rereleased in 1980?

6. Patsy was depicted in what film starring Sissy Spacek?

7. What Pasty Cline song did her friend Loretta Lynn record and have a #1 *Billboard* hit with in 1977?

8. Through modern recording technique Patsy's voice was rerecorded with the late Jim Reeves on what 1981 record?

9. Patsy's voice was heard on an Irving Berlin tune released in 1980. What was the song?

10. Complete these Patsy Cline song titles:
   "Sweet ——— ——— ———"
   "——— Love"
   "Leavin' ——— ——— ———"

69. JIM REEVES

1. Jim was born in the state of ———.

2. What baseball team signed Jim?

3. Although associated with RCA records for many years, Jim was initially recorded on a smaller label owned by Fabor Robinson. What was the label called?

4. Jim starred in what film about South Africa's diamond strike days?

5. On what live country music show was Jim a regular?

6. What person is dedicated to keeping Jim's memory and music alive, although he died in 1964?

7. Jim's very first release went to #1 on *Billboard*'s charts. What was it?

8. "He'll Have to Go" stayed on the country music charts longer than any other Reeves hit. What other distinction has the record?

9. What female vocalist has dubbed her voice over Jim's tapes for several new releases in the 1980's?

10. Complete these Jim Reeves song titles:
   "——— ——— ——— Sucker"
   "Am ——— ——— You"
   "Distant ———"

70. HANK WILLIAMS

1. Hank was born in ———.

2. Hank had great parallels with what other legendary country music singer?

3. Who portrayed Hank in the film on his life called *Your Cheatin' Heart*?

4. Whose voice was used for the singing parts of the film *Your Cheatin' Heart*?

5. For what major label did Hank record and who masterminded the Hank Williams sound on record?

6. What great inspirational song did Hank write and record?

7. What song was released, ironically, just before Hank died?

8. Hank, along with Fred Rose and Jimmie Rodgers, have what distinction with the CMA?

9. From 1953 through 1966 no Hank Williams songs appeared on the country charts, until one of Hank's most haunting melodies was released. What was it?

10. Complete these Hank Williams song titles, a meager sampling of the prolific writings and talents of the man many believe to be the greatest country music singer who ever lived.
    "——— It on ———"
    "Settin' ——— ——— ——— ———"
    "Take ——— ——— ——— ——— ———"
    "Half ——— Much"

71. HANK SNOW

1. Hank was born in ————.

2. What was Hank's 1950 hit that stayed on the charts for over forty weeks?

3. In addition to radio, records, and stage, Hank also had a fling in ————.

4. Hank is noted for the use of ———— on his suits.

5. In recent years Hank has conducted benefits to raise money for what cause?

6. With what record label has Hank been associated for over thirty years?

7. Hank added a singing partner to his show in the early 1980's. What is her name?

8. What is the song with the tongue-twisting lyric Hank recorded in 1962?

9. What singer did Hank admire so much that he named his eldest son after him and recorded many songs with a "train" theme?

10. Complete these Hank Snow song titles:
    "———— Boogie"
    "Music ———— ———— ———— Memphis"
    "I ———— ———— Anymore"

72. DOLLY PARTON

1. Dolly is from ————.

2. With whom did Dolly record and tour in the 1960's and 1970's?

3. As a songwriter Dolly has been very successful. Many of her songs reflect what background?

4. What two CMA awards has Dolly received?

5. What daring thing did Dolly do with her career in the late 1970's?

6. Dolly has been with RCA records since the 1960's. What label did Dolly previously record for?

7. Dolly's song "Joshua" has what distinction?

8. Dolly made her movie debut in a film for which she also wrote a highly successful theme. Who were her costars in the film?

9. Which of Dolly's songs probably reflects her mountain family background more than any other? It speaks of a certain item of clothing.

10. Complete these Dolly Parton song titles:
    "Love ———— ———— ———— Butterfly"
    "All ———— ———— ————"
    "———— Doors ————"

Answers to photo quiz section appear on pages 169–170.

1. Name the 1961 Tex Ritter hit about some of country music's deceased stars.

2. Kitty Wells is known as the "_____ of Country Music."

3. Roy Acuff is adept at playing with what toy?

4. In what film was Willie
Nelson featured with Jane
Fonda and Robert Redford?

5. What distinction has
Stonewall Jackson with the
Grand Ole Opry?

6. What was the name of Jim
Reeves' band?

7. What is the title of the novel written by Tom T. Hall?

8. Who gave Hank Williams, Jr., the nickname "Bocephus"?

9. Bill Anderson wrote and recorded "Tips of My Fingers," but it took what singer to make it a giant hit?

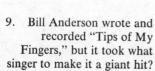

10. Charley Pride was discovered by what country music star?

11. Loretta Lynn is seen in TV and magazine ads pitching what product?

12. What association has Mel Tillis with Webb Pierce, Ray Price, Carl Smith, Little Jimmy Dickens, and Bobby Bare?

13. In what Texas town is Mickey Gilley's famous nightclub located?

14. Besides records, where else were you likely to have heard Janie Fricke's lovely voice?

15. By what title is Don Williams often called?

16. Is it true or false that Johnny Cash once served time in prison?

17. What 1960's pop/rock hit by Chuck Jackson did Ronnie Milsap remake into a hit in 1982?

18. Ricky Scaggs was a part of what star's band before striking out on his own?

19. Name Razzy Bailey's hit "truckin'" song.

20. Tammy Wynette gained exposure in her early career on what singer's syndicated TV show?

73. LORETTA LYNN

1. Loretta was born in the state of ———

2. Loretta was born in what town?

3. What country act gave Loretta a tremendous career boost?

4. Name Loretta's first successful record. Pat yourself on the back if you know what label it was on.

5. What entire town did Loretta and husband Mooney buy?

6. Name Loretta's first #1 *Billboard* chart hit record.

7. Loretta has won CMA "Female Vocalist of the Year" three times. What CMA award has she won four times?

8. Loretta once sang a duet on television with what well-known pop music legend?

9. What song tells it all about Loretta? It is her theme song, title of her autobiography, and title of the film based on the book.

10. Complete these Loretta Lynn song titles, just a sampling of the great songs that have flowed from the incredible mind, heart, and voice of this great country music star.

    "You're ——— ——— Country"
    "——— City"
    "One's ——— ——— ———"
    "Love ——— ——— Foundation"
    "Trouble ——— ———"

74. CONWAY TWITTY

1. Conway was born in the state of ———.

2. Conway gained initial fame in the 1950's as a rock 'n' roll singer. What was his most famous hit from that era?

3. What do these titles mean in Conway's background? *Platinum High School, Sex Kittens Go to College,* and *High School Confidential.*

4. Name Conway's first #1 record as a country singer.

5. Based on three major trade papers, Conway has had more #1 records than any other country artist. Guess how many.   a. 56   b. 22   c. 44

6. Where does the name Conway Twitty come from?

7. What is the name of Conway's vast entertainment complex opened in 1982 just outside Nashville?

8. What is the name of the bird that has become a familiar logo for for Conway?

9. Aside from winning the CMA "Vocal Duo of the Year" award with Loretta Lynn, what other CMA award has Conway won?

10. Complete these Conway Twitty song titles:
    "——— Darlin' "
    "——— ——— Ago"
    "——— ——— Jeans"

75. CHARLEY PRIDE

1. Charley was born in ———.

2. Charley's first #1 *Billboard*-charted record was ———?

3. At what job did Charley work with his family during childhood?

4. With what Hank Williams song did Charley enjoy success in the 1960's?

5. What CMA award did Charley win two years in a row?

6. Charley also won another CMA award in 1971. Name it.

7. What 1976 Charley Pride hit has become Charley's opening song in concert?

8. With what record label has Charley been associated his entire career?

9. Charley recorded a song in 1972 called "All His Children." What pop music artist is featured on the song?

10. Complete these Charley Pride song titles:
    "It's Gonna ——— ——— ——— ——— ———"
    "You're My ———"
    "Burgers and ———"

76. BUCK OWENS

1. Another singer from the great state of ———.

2. Buck's talents as an instrumentalist led him to what initial success and work in the recording industry?

3. Besides Susan Raye, what female singer has Buck recorded duets with?

4. Buck recorded in what California city, thus by-passing the "Nashville Sound"?

5. What song recorded by the Beatles was also recorded by Buck? What distinction does Buck's version have?

6. Buck has been a major contributor to the success of what TV show?

7. While CMA awards have eluded him personally, what awards have been bestowed upon his organization?

8. What animal did Buck have by the tail in one of his hit records?

9. What music industry trade paper was the subject of a Buck Owens hit record?

10. Complete these Buck Owens song titles:
    "——— Dark Stranger"
    "——— Your Spell ———"
    "——— Again"

77. WAYLON JENNINGS

1. Waylon claims ———— as his home state.

2. Waylon toured as electric bass player with what 1950's rock 'n' roll star?

3. Besides winning the CMA award for "Best Album of the Year" in 1976 (with other "Outlaws"), Waylon won what CMA award in 1975?

4. Waylon's frequently heard on records with what other singer?

5. Who was a guest on Waylon's first TV special?

6. Name the song recorded with Willie that had tremendous impact on a small town and was a smash hit.

7. Besides recording duets with his wife Jessi Colter, Waylon also recorded with what other female artist?

8. What was Waylon's first #1 *Billboard* hit?

9. In 1975 a Jennings single saluted two country music giants. Name them.

10. Complete these Waylon Jennings song titles:
    "Good ———— ————"
    "———— with ————"
    "I've Always ———— ————"

78. LYNN ANDERSON

1. Lynn claims ———— as her home state.

2. What did Lynn want you to listen to on one of her hit records?

3. What CMA award did Lynn walk away with in 1971?

4. Lynn's involvement in music has not decreased her love for what sport?

5. Who is Lynn's famous singing and songwriting mother?

6. On whose television show was Lynn featured in 1970?

7. What Osborne Brothers song did Lynn record in 1970?

8. A Johnny Ray song from the 1950's was turned into a hit by Lynn in 1972. What was it?

9. Lynn's last #1 *Billboard*-charted record was in 1974. What was it called?

10. Complete these Lynn Anderson song titles:
    "You're ———— ————"
    "How ———— ———— ———— ————"
    "Top ———— ———— ————"

79. MICKEY GILLEY

1. Mickey was born in the state of ———.

2. What old George Morgan song did Mickey record that was his first real hit?

3. Mickey is a cousin to what other country music star?

4. In what film were Mickey Gilley songs featured that helped to spawn a craze named after the film?

5. What craze was Mickey responsible for starting through his Texas nightclub?

6. In 1980 Mickey had two #1 *Billboard* hits in a row and in the same month. Both songs were former rock 'n' roll hits. Name them.

7. Mickey has had two hit records with roses in the title. Name another Gilley hit with another flower in the title.

8. In 1975 Mickey recorded a duet that met with moderate success. Who sings with Mickey on this duet?

9. On what network TV show did Mickey have a dramatic role in the 1981–1982 season?

10. Complete these Mickey Gilley song titles:
    "Don't —— —— —— —— —— —— Time"
    "—— —— Memories"
    "—— Sensation"

80. TAMMY WYNETTE

1. Tammy was born in —————.

2. At what occupation did Tammy work before striking it big in country music?

3. For what label has Tammy recorded her entire career?

4. What distinction in record sales does Tammy hold?

5. What Tammy Wynette hit was written in part by Johnny Paycheck?

6. What was Tammy's first #1 hit?

7. Some of Tammy's songs have seemed autobiographical in nature. Name the 1968 hit by Tammy in which a word is spelled out rather than spoken, so a child will not know the subject of the conversation.

8. What was the first George and Tammy #1 record?

9. What early 1950's song, once a theme for Milton Berle, did George and Tammy record in 1976?

10. Complete these Tammy Wynette song titles:
    "Til ——— ——— ——— ——— ——— ———"
    "He ——— ——— ——— ——— ———"
    "——— to ———"

81. MERLE HAGGARD

1. Merle was born in the state of ———.

2. What connection has Ronald Reagan with Merle's life?

3. Who was Leonard in the hit record by Haggard of 1981?

4. Merle was once married to the ex-wife of a country music star who helped him in the recording business. What is her name?

5. Name one of Merle's fascinations which led him to record a concept album on the subject.

6. With what movie star did Merle record a 1980 record?

7. What record and song by Merle created quite a stir in 1970, given the mood of the country?

8. Merle appeared on what singer's last album?

9. What song did Merle record about Elvis that was included in a tribute album to "The King"? The album was recorded before Elvis's death.

10. Complete these Haggard song titles:
    "It's Been ——— ——— ———"
    "If ——— ——— ——— ——— ———"
    "I Think ——— ——— ——— ——— ——— ———"

82. SONNY JAMES

1. Sonny was born in what state?

2. What song recorded by Sonny was also a big pop music hit for Tab Hunter?

3. In 1967 Sonny made a film called *Hillbilly in a Haunted House*. Can you name the famous man of a thousand faces who was also starred in the film?

4. From 1967 through 1971 Sonny achieved a remarkable feat on the country music charts. What was it?

5. Sonny has had an interesting source for some of the hit records he's had. What is it?

6. What is unique about one of Sonny's albums?

7. For what label did Sonny record until 1972?

8. What slight edge on show business did Sonny have as a child?

9. Sonny's first #1 *Billboard* hit was a remake originally done by pop singer Adam Wade. What was the name of the song?

10. Complete these Sonny James song titles:
    "First ——, First ——, First ——"
    "When Something —— —— —— —— ——"
    "A Little Bit —— —— ——"

83. WHO AM I?

1. I was born in Tennessee.

2. I was a regular on WROL in Knoxville, went into the Navy, then came back to WROL in the late 1940's.

3. My debut on the "Grand Ole Opry" was in 1950.

4. I had a weekly show on Canadian TV in the mid-1960's.

5. *The Badge of Marshall Brennan* and *Buffalo Guns* are two movies I made.

6. For twenty-four years I recorded with Columbia records.

7. My first wife was June Carter, my second wife is Goldie Hill.

8. In 1951 I was named #1 country singer by major country music polls.

9. I was featured on an ABC show called *Four Star Jubilee.*

10. Joe Stampley and Moe Bandy rerecorded one of my hits in the early 1980's.

84. WHO AM I?

1. I was born in Arkansas.

2. My career started as a studio musician backing many of the major recording stars of the day.

3. I was part of a group called the Champs that recorded a hit called "Tequila."

4. In the movies I was a co-star with the immortal John Wayne in a film called *True Grit*.

5. Songwriters whose songs I have recorded include John Hartford and Jimmy Webb.

6. I have recorded duets with female singers Anne Murray, Bobbie Gentry, Tanya Tucker, and Rita Coolidge.

7. I host a major PGA golf tournament.

8. I was a two-time CMA award winner in 1968 for "Entertainer of the Year" and "Male Vocalist of the Year."

9. I played bagpipes on one of my records.

10. Complete some of my song titles:
    "Dreams of —— —— ——"
    "Gentle —— —— ——"
    "By the —— —— —— —— ——"

85. GEORGE JONES

1. George was born in the state of ———.

2. Name at least two record labels George has recorded for over the years besides Epic.

3. With what rock 'n' roll singer did George record, but with only moderate success?

4. Aside from Tammy, name at least two other females George has recorded duets with.

5. In 1959 George had a #1 *Billboard* hit, his first. It was about something you drink. What was it called?

6. Besides being named "Song of the Year" (a writer's award), what other CMA award did "He Stopped Loving Her Today" win?

7. What artist recorded a 1980 duet album with George called, *Double Trouble*?

8. The Oak Ridge Boys backed George on what 1982 hit?

9. Name George's favorite song of those he has recorded.

10. Complete these George Jones song titles:
    "Who ——— ———"
    "——— Blues"
    "Walk ——— ——— ——— ——— Me"

86. WHO AM I?

1. I was born in the state of Louisiana.

2. My band once included artists such as Faron Young and Floyd Cramer.

3. I was once a member of the Louisiana Hayride.

4. My first #1 *Billboard* hit came in 1952 with a song called "Back Street Affair."

5. A guitar-shaped swimming pool at my Nashville residence caused quite a stir with some of my neighbors in the 1970's.

6. Several of my hit songs have been written by Mel Tillis.

7. I won many awards in the early 1950's from various organizations, including the Jukebox Operators.

8. Some of my hits have been my own compositions.

9. Prior to hitting it big in the music business I worked as a salesman for Sears.

10. Some of my hits include:
    "Slowly"
    "More and More"
    "There Stands a Glass"

87. DON GIBSON

1. His home state is ———.

2. His base of operations in the 1940's was ———, where he was featured on WNOX Radio.

3. Don's main interest early in his career was in song-writing. What hit did he write for Faron Young?

4. What country classic did Don write that was a hit first for Kitty Wells and has since been recorded by dozens of artists?

5. What Don Gibson song was one of 1958's biggest records and established him as a top performer as well as songwriter?

6. Ronnie Milsap recorded what Don Gibson song in 1974?

7. Don recorded duets with what two females?

8. What kind of day did Don have in his 1958 hit record?

9. Don recorded a Hank Snow hit in 1959. Name it.

10. Complete these Don Gibson song titles:
    "Give ——— ——— ———"
    "Just ——— ———"
    "Woman ——— ———"

88. OAK RIDGE BOYS

1. In what sport do several of the Oak Ridge Boys have an ownership interest?

2. Name the group's four members.

3. For years the group's major thrust was in what type of music?

4. What is the record that moved the Oak Ridge Boys into mainstream country music?

5. What CMA award did the group capture for one year from the Statler Brothers?

6. Name the incredibly successful hit that took CMA "Single of the Year" honors for the Oaks in 1981.

7. What are the names of the two buses the group travels in on tour?

8. In 1981 the Oak Ridge Boys were spokespersons for what organization?

9. The Oak Ridge Boys recorded a song with a girl's name in the title that was a hit in 1982. What was it?

10. Complete these Oak Ridge Boys song titles:
    "Heart —— ——"
    "—— Louisiana —— —— —— Daylight"
    "I'll —— —— —— You"

89. MISCELLANEOUS

1. I wrote a hit for the Oak Ridge Boys called "Leavin' Lousiana in the Broad Daylight," had several moderately successful records in the early 1980's, and am married to Rosanne Cash. Who am I?

2. My voice has been heard on dozens of radio and TV commercials, and I once worked as a secretary in Nashville. I've also done extensive back-up singing work and I've had hit records like "Down to My Last Broken Heart" and "Pass Me By." Who am I?

3. My hits have included an old Lefty Frizzell song and a song about a year in the late 1950's. I did an album called "I Just Came Home to Count the Memories." Who am I?

4. Our first names are Royce and Jeannie, we're the ————.

5. I've written many songs, including "Joy to the World" and one about someone working very hard. I've also starred on TV and in movies such as *The Black Stallion*. Who am I?

6. In the 1950's a song I recorded about a candy bar and a flower was a giant hit in the pop field. Then I was on the country charts. I'm very popular in England. Who am I?

7. Once I was married to Ralph Emery. Once I recorded a song called "End of the World." Now I am a member of the "Grand Ole Opry." Who am I?

8. "Patches" was a big pop hit for me in 1962. Now I'm

strictly country with hits such as "9,999,999 Tears" and "Rocky." Who am I?

9. Mine has been a seemingly meteoric rise to fame in country music. My first release was a giant hit called, "Somebody's Knockin'." I'm a Georgian. Who am I?

10. A song about glasses tinted a certain color and an old Ray Charles song are two of my hits. I also did a song about a person reaching a certain age in life. Who am I?

90. MISCELLANEOUS

1. My dad was a singing cowboy and I'm trying to carry on the tradition. I've recorded duets with Margo Smith and hosted an "on location" TV show called *Nashville on the Road*. Who am I?

2. I've recorded with Joe, and rodeo life has played a background in my life and music. One of my early hits was about the music of Hank Williams. Who am I?

3. A hit of mine was the basis for a movie. I'm considered a country music "outlaw." Another hit for me was about the IRS. Who am I?

4. We're brothers from Texas with many hit records. Need you know more?

5. I'm from Birmingham, Alabama, and once worked as a waitress while trying to get established in the music business. I won the CMA "Female Vocalist of the Year" award in 1980. Who am I?

6. Legend has it my sister named me after a fast food restaurant in Nashville. My hits list is long and so is my hair! Who am I?

7. We're one of country's hottest groups. Three of us are cousins. We won the CMA "Vocal Group of the Year" award in 1981 and cleaned up at the Academy of Country Music's awards show in 1982. Who are we?

8. I won the very first "Single of the Year" award given by the CMA in 1967. Jeannie Seely and I were sing-

ing partners. I was also first recipient of the CMA's "Male Vocalist of the Year" award. Who am I?

9. Nova Scotia's my home. I rerecorded a George Jones song. Many of my records have been country and pop hits, such as "You Needed Me." Who am I?

10. Two of my biggest records were "Gone" and "Wings of a Dove." I also went by the name of Terry Preston for a while. Who am I?

91. DAVID HOUSTON

1. David was born in the state of ————.

2. David was a member of what popular radio show?

3. What vocal technique does David have that is nearly extinct in today's country music?

4. What have the titles *Cottonpickin' Chickenpickers* and *Horse Soldiers* to do with David?

5. Name the song that earned David two Grammy awards.

6. Besides Barbara Mandrell, what female artist has David recorded with?

7. David is a cousin of what country music singer?

8. David has famous ancestors. Name at least one of his famous relatives.

9. David's first release on Epic Records was a top-ten hit in 1963. Can you name it?

10. Complete these David Houston song titles:
    "With ———— ————"
    "Have ———— ———— Faith"
    "———— Things"

92. JERRY LEE LEWIS

1. Jerry Lee was born in what state?

2. Jerry's first charted record was both a country and a pop hit. Name it.

3. Name a film in which Jerry Lee was featured with Conway Twitty and for which Jerry Lee wrote the title song.

4. In 1968 "The Killer" played a role in a rock 'n' roll musical version of what Shakespeare play?

5. Jerry Lee went exclusively country, with his rockin' piano style still evident, in the late 1960's and scored a #1 *Billboard* chart topper in 1972 with a remake of what 1950's hit?

6. What 1977 hit by Jerry Lee reflected a man's reaching a certain point in life?

7. Name the Judy Garland song given "The Killer's" treatment in 1980.

8. In 1969 Jerry Lee recorded a top-ten duet called "Don't Let Me Cross Over" with what female artist?

9. Name another country/rock 'n' roll classic that was a hit for Jerry Lee in 1957.

10. Complete these Jerry Lee Lewis song titles:
      "Drinkin' —— —— ——"
      "Who's —— —— —— —— Piano"
      "What's —— Milwaukee ——"

93. HANK THOMPSON

1. Hank was born in ———.

2. What "singing cowboy" gave Hank a helping hand in the 1940's?

3. In addition to being a fine singer, Hank is also talented in what area?

4. From the 1950's to the 1960's what distinction did Hank's band achieve?

5. How did Hank like his drink in a 1968 record Hank recorded for Dot Records?

6. Name the song Hank did in 1958 that had a strange lyric line reflective of the dog teams in Alaska?

7. In 1960 Hank had a hit with a song about something "to go." What was he referring to?

8. One of Hank's records crossed over into pop in 1960. Name it.

9. What group had a pop hit with a Hank Thompson record called "Cab Driver"?

10. Complete these Hank Thompson song titles:
    "Whoa ———"
    "The Older the ———, ——— Sweeter the ———"
    "Smokey ——— ———"

94. ELVIS

1. Name one of Elvis's early records that was a treatment of a song previously done by Bill Monroe.

2. What was the first Elvis record to hit the country music charts?

3. For how much did Sam Phillips sell Elvis to RCA Records?

4. What was the name of the group that backed Elvis on many of his early records?

5. Name Elvis's first movie.

6. Who were the two instrumentalists who backed Elvis during his early days?

7. Who was Elvis's manager and what country artist was also managed by this person for a while?

8. Name Elvis's first #1 record on the *Billboard* country charts.

9. After not being on the charts since 1958, name the song that was a top-ten hit for Elvis in 1971.

10. What was unique about Elvis's early appearances on television?

95. ROGER MILLER

1. Another country music singer from the state of _____.

2. Roger's an excellent songwriter. What artist recorded a song written by Roger that gave Roger his first big break? It was a song called "Invitation to the Blues."

3. Roger provided the voice for a character in what Walt Disney cartoon movie?

4. In 1965 Roger set a precedent by winning what award how many times?

5. What Roger Miller song was rerecorded in the early 1980's by David Frizzell and Shelly West?

6. With what hit song is Roger very closely identified?

7. What distinction did many of Rogers's records achieve in the music world?

8. What was the number of the engine Roger wrote and sang about in his 1965 record?

9. Roger's career received a boost by appearances on the TV show of what pop singer?

10. Complete these Roger Miller song titles:
    "____ Me"
    "You Can't ____ ____ ____ ____ ____ Herd"
    "One ____ and ____ ____"

96. ROY CLARK

1. Roy's home state is ————.

2. Roy was associated with what other country music star on a TV show out of Washington, D.C.?

3. What championship did Roy win two years in a row back in the 1940's?

4. Roy appeared with and provided backup on records for what female star?

5. Roy also performed as a featured act with what other artist?

6. Name the "picker" with whom Roy took the CMA's "Instrumental Group of the Year" award in 1975 and 1976.

7. In 1973 Roy was voted what award by the CMA?

8. What kind of drink did Roy "pitch" on TV commercials?

9. Roy was the first country music star to be host of what popular TV show?

10. Complete these Roy Clark song titles:
    "Tips ———— ———— ————"
    "———— ———— ———— ———— Young"
    "Thank ———— ———— Greyhound"

97. MISCELLANEOUS

1. The lead singer in this trio once was part of a group that backed Elvis on tours. Their first hit was in 1975, a song called "Queen of the Silver Dollar."

2. His voice is pure country and in the early 1980's he underwent an image change with a new hair style and beard. His "Farewell Party" was a hit in 1979.

3. She was in her teens when she first burst on the country music scene. She was romantically linked with Glen Campbell for a while. One of her hits was "Delta Dawn."

4. This northern boy has an Irish background and writes nearly all of his material with partners Even Stevens and David Malloy. One of the songs he wrote, "Kentucky Rain," was an Elvis hit.

5. What entertainer had his first charted record in the country music field at the age of eighty-three?

6. His first charted record was in 1976, but it did poorly. Since then he has emerged as a chart contender for the 1980's with hits such as "Lovin' Up a Storm" and "True Life Country Music."

7. In concert he displays a flashy "Elvis" style. He was introduced in 1959 with a lot of hype as a new rock 'n' roll star, but only had one charted record. He's been far more successful in country music with hits such as "Rub It In."

8. At one time she modeled swimsuits and casual fashions for a major department store. Now this pretty

gal makes hit records such as "Who's Cheatin' Who" and "Men."

9. This handsome singer's tribute record to Elvis in 1977 established his career. His follow-up records were strong enough to keep him on top.

10. Her songs "Queen of Hearts" and "The Sweetest Thing" were hits that helped earn her the Academy of Country Music's "Most Promising Female" award in 1982.

98. WHO AM I?

1. I was born in Arkansas.

2. In the 1960's I hit the pop/rock charts with songs like "Lonely Weekends" and "Mohair Sam."

3. During my career in its early stages I was associated with Sam Phillips and Sun Records.

4. Another influence on my style was Shelby Singleton.

5. In 1973 I was voted "Male Vocalist of the Year" by the CMA.

6. Also in 1973 a hit record of mine was voted "Single of the Year." The song also won an award for its writer, Kenny O'Dell.

7. In 1974 the most coveted of all CMA awards, "Entertainer of the Year," was bestowed upon me.

8. I was white-haired by age thirty-three, which accounts for my nickname.

9. I had a #1 *Billboard*-charted duet with Janie Fricke in 1978, called "On My Knees."

10. Complete some of my song titles:
    "—— Closed ——"
    "The —— Beautiful ——"
    "There —— —— Anymore"

99. MISCELLANEOUS

1. My father was "the" country music legend and I've immortalized him in several of my songs. I've never tried to sound like him because I have my own distinct style. "Family Tradition" was one of my hits. Who am I?

2. I'm a football player who loves country music and I had a charted record in 1980, although it didn't do very well. Who am I?

3. My special TV record packages have sold phenomenally well, although I've never had a giant hit record. They love me in England. Who am I?

4. My first #1 *Billboard*-charted record was in 1980 with "One Day at a Time." Who am I?

5. I can only be seen in performance with a mask to hide my face. I sound a lot like Elvis and have had moderately successful records. Who am I?

6. My really big hit was about a certain type of bed covering, although I have managed to bounce back since that 1973 hit with other top-ten records. Who am I?

7. The special TV record packages of my hits caused a new interest in my career in the early 1980's. Before that my career had been in limbo. I had lots of hit records in the 1950's. Who am I?

8. My father is one of country's greats. In 1981 I had a hit record called "My Baby Thinks He's a Train." My husband is involved in music too. Who am I?

9. I am one of country music's "stars of the 80's," al-

though I've worked long and hard to achieve status in the business. My hits have included "Hard Times" and "Hillbilly Girl with the Blues." Who am I?

10. My cousins are Jimmy Seals of Seals and Crofts and Danny Seals of England Dan and John Ford Coley. One of my biggest hits was a duet with Janie Fricke. Who am I?

100. MISCELLANEOUS

1. I've written songs for many artists and toured with Charley Pride. Dean Dillon and I got together on an album in 1982. One of my hits was "She's Acting Single (and I'm Drinking Doubles)." Who am I?

2. Most of my early hits went only on the pop charts, although my roots have always been in country music. Red Foley gave me a big career boost. A more recent hit of mine was made with the Oak Ridge Boys backing me. Who am I?

3. In 1964 a song Bill Anderson wrote called "Once A Day" was a big hit for me. I've been in country-music-oriented movies. I'm a current "Grand Ole Opry" member and have very deep religious convictions. Who am I?

4. I started in pop music then hit it big in country, where my top records have included "If You Touch Me" and "Soul Song." Moe and I are just "Good Ole Boys." Who am I?

5. With a d.j. buddy I formed my own label called Cimmaron and had a top-ten hit in 1973. It was called "Drift Away." My high falsetto voice has been heard on songs such as "Lonely Teardrops" and "My Prayer." Who am I?

6. A song I wrote and recorded in 1958 was released under the name Bill Parsons. A song I helped to adapt from a French melody became a hit for me called "500 Miles Away from Home." My record "New Cut Road" was a hit in 1982. Who am I?

7. My hits include "Ann (Don't Go Running)" and "If Love Was a Bottle of Wine." For a while I called myself Tommy Dean from Abilene. I once managed Dot Records' Nashville office. Who am I?

8. Two hits of mine are "Wasted Days and Wasted Nights" and "Before the Next Teardrop Falls." Who am I?

9. I did a song about a certain year and model of car. Other hits of mine included "Blanket on the Ground" and "What I've Got in Mind." Who am I?

10. I've been very successful on Canadian television and I spend time in a nightclub on Printer's Alley in Nashville. I'm a singer, comedian, and instrumentalist. My character "Harold the Horny Toad" is quite popular. Who am I?

ANSWER
SECTION

1. GRAND OLE OPRY

1. *WSM Barn Dance*
2. The "Solemn Ole Judge," George D. Hay
3. Uncle Dave Macon
4. A six-foot oval section from the stage of the Ryman is built-in near the footlights at center-stage at the new "Grand Ole Opry" house. Performers get the feeling of actually being on stage at the old Ryman Auditorium.
5. Elvis Presley, according to legend.
6. NBC
7. President Richard M. Nixon
8. Stringbean. His wife Estelle was also murdered. Robbery was the motive, as the comedian always carried large sums of money with him.
9. Roy Acuff
10. The "Camel Caravan," which toured all over the country with "Grand Ole Opry" stars.

2. COUNTRY STARS AND THEIR NICKNAMES

1. Marty Robbins
2. Bill Anderson
3. Jimmie Rodgers
4. Eddy Arnold
5. Jerry Lee Lewis
6. George Jones
7. Jim Reeves
8. Ray Price
9. Charlie Rich
10. Rex Allen

3. NATIONAL BARN DANCES

1. Wheeling, West Virginia
2. Chicago, Illinois
3. Shreveport, Louisiana
4. Chicago, Illinois (WGN picked up *Barn Dance* in 1960 when WLS dropped it)
5. Roanoke, Virginia
6. Dallas, Texas
7. Little Rock, Arkansas
8. Knoxville, Tennessee
9. Cincinnati, Ohio
10. Arlington, Virginia

4. MATCH REAL NAME WITH STAR'S STAGE NAME

1. e
2. c
3. g
4. f
5. d
6. h
7. b
8. j
9. i
10. a

5. NAME THE "COUNTRY COMICS"

1. Minnie Pearl
2. Stringbean
3. Lonzo and Oscar
4. Jerry Clower
5. Homer and Jethro
6. Archie Campbell
7. Duke of Paducah (Whitey Ford)
8. Judy Canova
9. Junior Samples
10. Rod Brasfield

6. COUNTRY RELATIVES

1. (West) Mother and daughter
2. (Frizzell) Brothers
3. (Owens) Father and son
4. (Parton) Sisters
5. (Tucker) Sisters
6. (Anderson) Mother and daughter
7. (Tubb) Father and son
8. (Cooper) Mother and daughter
9. (Cash) Father and daughter
10. (Wright) Father and son

7. TIME OUT TO UNSCRAMBLE

1. Jerry Lee Lewis
2. Loretta Lynn
3. Johnny Cash
4. Hank Snow
5. Elvis Presley
6. Ricky Scaggs
7. Carl Perkins
8. John Anderson
9. Charlie Rich
10. Gail Davies

Lewis, Cash, Presley, Perkins, and Rich each recorded on the Sun Record label out of Memphis in the 1950's.

8. REAL FIRST NAMES

1. Foley
2. Locklin
3. King
4. Owens
5. Rodriguez
6. Snow
7. Sovine
8. Whitman
9. Frizzell
10. Copas

9. MORE . . . MATCH REAL NAME WITH SINGER'S STAGE NAME

1. e
2. g
3. h
4. d
5. i
6. c
7. a
8. b
9. f
10. j

10. MATCH BANDS WITH THEIR LEADERS

1. b
2. f
3. g
4. h
5. i
6. j
7. c
8. a
9. e
10. d

11. COVERS OF COUNTRY HITS

1. Frankie Laine
2. Guy Mitchell
3. Rosemary Clooney
4. Guy Mitchell
5. Patti Page
6. Rosemary Clooney
7. Eddie Fisher
8. Frankie Laine
9. Perry Como
10. Tony Bennett

12. MISCELLANEOUS

1. "Fan Fair"
2. De Ford Bailey
3. Olivia Newton-John
4. It was made the state song of Arizona.
5. Mac Davis
6. Norma Jean
7. "Jamboree in the Hills"
8. Jim Ed Brown
9. Mary Kay Place, who starred on *Mary Hartman, Mary Hartman*
10. Mother Maybelle Carter

13. NETWORK COUNTRY MUSIC TV SHOWS

1. *Johnny Cash Show*
2. *Music Country U.S.A.*
3. *The Barbara Mandrell Show*
4. *Ozark Jubilee, Country Music Jubilee,* or *Jubilee U.S.A.*
5. *The Eddy Arnold Show*
6. Snooky Lanson, Tex Ritter, Jimmy Wakely, Carl Smith, and Rex Allen
7. *Midwestern Hayride*
8. *The Glen Campbell Goodtime Hour*
9. *Hee Haw*
10. "Grand Ole Opry"

14. FAMOUS COUNTRY DUETS

1. Jan Howard (1971)
2. Priscilla Mitchell (1965)
3. Betty Foley (1955)
4. Jeannie Seely (1969)
5. Helen Cornelius (1980)
6. Jessi Colter (1970 and 1976)
7. Margo Smith (1980)
8. Waylon Jennings (1978)
9. Barbara Mandrell (1970)
10. Melba Montgomery (1965)

15. SONGS ABOUT ROSES

1. "Bouquet of Roses"
2. "Angels and Rain"
3. "Eleven Roses"
4. "When the Snow Is on the Roses"
5. "Roses for Mama"
6. "Room Full of Roses"
7. "I Never Promised You a Rose Garden"
8. "Paper Roses"
9. "Roses and Love Songs"
10. "Send Me No Roses"

16. MORE . . . MATCH BANDS WITH THEIR LEADERS

1. d
2. f
3. h
4. g
5. b
6. c
7. a
8. j
9. i
10. e

17. MORE...NETWORK COUNTRY MUSIC TV SHOWS

1. *The Jerry Reed When You're Hot You're Hot Hour*
2. *The Jimmy Dean Show*
3. *ABC Barn Dance,* or *National Barn Dance*
4. The Everly Brothers
5. *Hayloft Hoedown*
6. Pee Wee King
7. *The Ford Show starring Tennessee Ernie Ford*
8. *The Roy Rogers and Dale Evans Show*
9. *Village Barn*
10. *Saturday Night Jamboree*

18. COUNTRY INSTRUMENTALISTS

1. f
2. h
3. e
4. c
5. j
6. i
7. a
8. g
9. d
10. b

19. MATCH THE SINGER WITH HIS—OR HER—HIT SONG

1. d
2. e
3. f
4. b
5. i
6. j
7. a
8. h
9. g
10. c

20. ROCK 'N' ROLL AND COUNTRY

1. "Chantilly Lace"
2. The Platters
3. Connie Smith
4. Charlie Rich and Con Hunley
5. Ivory Joe Hunter
6. Narvel Felts and Billy Walker
7. "Hurt"
8. Buddy Holly
9. "Love Is Strange"
10. "Misty"

21. SINGING COWBOYS

RIS-OR HER-HIT SONG

1. Tex Ritter
2. Roy Rogers
3. Jimmy Wakely
4. Ray Whitely
5. Tex Williams
6. Rex Allen
7. Gene Autry
8. Spade Cooley
9. Ken Maynard
10. Johnny Bond

22. ANOTHER ROUND OF MATCH THE SINGER WITH THE HIT SONG

1. d
2. g
3. e
4. f
5. j
6. c
7. h
8. i
9. b
10. a

23. UNSCRAMBLE TIME

1. Bill Anderson
2. Tanya Tucker
3. Roy Acuff
4. Bob Luman
5. Charley Pride
6. Charlie Daniels
7. Jim Reeves
8. Glen Campbell
9. Buck Owens
10. Conway Twitty

Anderson, Luman, Acuff, Pride, Reeves, and Twitty were headed toward careers in professional baseball.

24. MORE ROCK 'N' ROLL AND COUNTRY

1. f or j
2. h
3. b
4. i
5. a
6. c
7. d
8. e
9. j or f
10. g

25. TV AND MOVIE THEMES ...
"COUNTRY STYLE"

1. *Movin' On*
2. "Take This Job and Shove It"
3. *"The Rebel,"* Nick Adams
4. Tex Ritter
5. Eddie Rabbitt
6. *Dukes of Hazzard*
7. *The Hangin' Tree*
8. Lester Flatt and Earl Scruggs, "Ballad of Jed Clampett"
9. Dolly Parton, *9 to 5*
10. *Petticoat Junction*

26. TRUCK DRIVIN' SINGERS AND
SONGS

1. Glen Campbell
2. A chicken truck
3. "Roll On, Big Mama"
4. "Teddy Bear"
5. "Convoy"
6. Dave Dudley
7. Norma Jean
8. George Hamilton IV
9. "Six Days on the Road"
10. Red Simpson

27. MATCH 'EM UP, PARTNER!

1. d
2. f
3. a
4. b
5. g
6. i
7. e
8. j
9. h
10. c

They all were disc jockeys or radio announcers prior to their success in country music.

28. MORE MATCH THE SINGER WITH THE HIT SONG

1. g
2. e
3. f
4. c
5. a
6. i
7. b
8. d
9. j
10. h

132

29. FROM THE SIDELINES TO STARDOM

1. e
2. h
3. d
4. j
5. c
6. b
7. f
8. i
9. a
10. g

30. COUNTRY MUSIC DATES

1. November 5, 1960
2. December 10, 1927
3. August 1, 1927
4. January 1, 1953
5. September 28, 1928
6. March 5, 1963
7. March 16, 1974
8. July 31, 1964
9. May 26, 1933
10. September 15, 1903

31. COUNTRY NOVELTY SONGS AND ARTISTS

1. "Shriner's Convention"
2. Homer and Jethro and "That Hound Dog in the Window"
3. Simon Crum
4. "The Streak"
5. Sheb Wooley
6. "Squirelly"
7. "Hello Walls"
8. "Baby, It's Cold Outside"
9. "Almost Persuaded"
10. "Battle of Kookamonga"

32. MORE ROCK 'N' ROLL AND COUNTRY

1. e
2. h
3. a
4. j
5. b
6. c
7. i
8. d
9. f
10. g

33. COUNTRY MUSIC ASSOCIATION AWARDS

1. The awards are presented every October, which is Country Music Month.
2. Kraft Foods
3. Loretta Lynn (1972)
4. Barbara Mandrell (1980 and 1981)
5. Dolly Parton
6. Comedian of the Year (award dropped in 1971)
7. Each won "Male Vocalist of the Year" in two consecutive years. (Charley 1971 and 1972, Ronnie 1976 and 1977, and George 1980 and 1981).
8. Terri Gibbs
9. Chet Atkins
10. Conway Twitty and Loretta Lynn

34. MORE COUNTRY MUSIC ASSOCIATION AWARDS

1. Statler Brothers
2. 1976—Waylon Jennings and Willie Nelson
   1980—Moe Bandy and Joe Stampley
3. Danny Davis and the Nashville Brass
4. Dottie West with Kenny Roberts won "Vocal Duo of the Year" in 1978 and 1979. In 1981 Dottie's daughter Shelly West won the same award with her partner David Frizzell.

5. "Easy Lovin' " in 1971 and 1972
   "He Stopped Lovin' Her Today" in 1980 and 1981
6. "Lucille" and "The Gambler"
7. Ronnie Milsap in 1975 (*Legend in My Time*), 1977 (*Ronnie Milsap Live*), and 1978 (*It Was Almost Like a Song*)
8. Johnny Cash for "Entertainer of the Year," "Male Vocalist of the Year," "Vocal Group of the Year" (with June Carter), "Single of the Year" ("A Boy Named Sue"), and "Album of the Year" (Johnny Cash at San Quentin Prison).
9. Ronnie Milsap
10. Tammy Wynette

35. MATCH THE SINGER WITH THE HIT SONG

1. f
2. h
3. e
4. b
5. g
6. c
7. i
8. a
9. j
10. d

36. FAMOUS COUNTRY BROTHERS

1. McGee (of the Fruit Jar Drinkers)
2. McReynolds
3. Reid (of the Statler Brothers)
4. Gatlin
5. Monroe
6. Bellamy
7. Glaser
8. Wilburn
9. Louvin
10. Carlisle

37. ROCK 'N' ROLL AND COUNTRY CONTINUED

1. Dolly Parton
2. The Chordettes
3. Dickey Lee
4. Margo Smith
5. Johnny Paycheck and George Jones
6. "Ain't That a Shame"
7. Glen Campbell
8. Brook Benton
9. Glen Campbell and Bobbie Gentry
10. Sonny James

38. SINGING HUSBANDS AND WIVES

1. Louise Mandrell and R. C. Bannon
2. Johnny Cash and June Carter Cash
3. Waylon Jennings and Jessi Colter
4. Tammy Wynette and George Jones
5. Kitty Wells and Johnny Wright
6. Merle Haggard and Leona Williams
7. Wilma Lee and Stoney Cooper
8. Jack Blanchard and Misty Morgan
9. Bonnie Owens and Merle Haggard
10. Carl Smith and Goldie Hill

39. MISCELLANEOUS TRIVIA

1. B. J. Thomas
2. "*Music City News* Awards" in June and the "Academy of Country Music Awards" in April.
3. *Maverick*, 1981–1982 season
4. *Nashville 99*, 1977
5. Leon Everette
6. Charlie Daniels
7. Texas
8. John Denver
9. They are all country music disc jockeys who have won the "DJ of the Year" award given yearly by the CMA.
10. Paul Revere and the Raiders

40. SONGS WITH A CITY TITLE

1. e
2. j
3. f
4. a
5. b
6. i
7. c
8. d
9. g
10. h

41. A COUNTRY CHRISTMAS

1. "Rockin' Around the Christmas Tree"
2. "Rudolph, the Red-Nosed Reindeer"
3. Eddy Arnold
4. Gene Autry
5. "Jingle Bell Rock"
6. Ernest Tubb
7. "Here Comes Santa Claus"
8. Elvis Presley
9. Ernest Tubb
10. Eddy Arnold

42. SONGS WITH A CITY TITLE, PART TWO

1. j
2. e
3. i
4. f
5. a
6. h
7. c
8. d
9. g
10. b

43. ANSWER SONGS

1. "It Wasn't God Who Made Honky Tonk Angels," Kitty Wells
2. Ben Colder ("Almost Persuaded #2")
3. "Queen of the House"
4. "He'll Have to Stay"
5. "Teddy Bear's Last Ride"
6. "I'm the Girl on Wolverton Mountain"
7. "Hello Walls"
8. Hank Locklin
9. Paul Anka
10. "Harper Valley P.T.A. (Later That Same Day)"

44. NASHVILLE AND TENNESSEE SONGS

1. e
2. g
3. f
4. b
5. c
6. i or d
7. d or i
8. h
9. a
   Both are official Tennessee state songs. There are five Tennessee state songs in all.

45. MATCH THE NICKNAME WITH THE STAR

1. e
2. f
3. i
4. h
5. j
6. a
7. c
8. b
9. d
10. g

46. ANOTHER ROUND OF ROCK 'N' ROLL AND COUNTRY

1. Vern Gosdin
2. The Cascades
3. "Save the Last Dance for Me"
4. Al Hibbler
5. "Walk Right Back"
6. Lynn Anderson
7. "Lonely Street"
8. Willie Nelson and Leon Russell
9. "Maybelline"
10. Margo Smith

47. FORMER OCCUPATIONS MATCH

1. e
2. f
3. g
4. b
5. c
6. d
7. h
8. i
9. j
10. a

48. SONGS WITH A CITY TITLE, PART THREE

1. f
2. g
3. e
4. i
5. a
6. b
7. j
8. c
9. d
10. h

49. COUNTRY POLITICS AND BOOKS

1. *Sing Me Back Home*
2. Governor of Tennessee
3. *From Harper Valley to the Mountain Top*
4. Jimmie Davis
5. *Stand By Your Man*
6. U.S. senator
7. *Man in Black*
8. Mayor
9. Hank Williams, Jr.
10. Stuart Hamblen

50. MISCELLANEOUS

1. Johnny Cash
2. Freddy Hart
3. Ernest Tubb
4. Oak Ridge Boys
5. Harold Reid of the Statler Brothers
6. Barbara Eden
7. Jimmie Rodgers and the Carter Family
8. Dottie West; she wrote a song used as a commercial theme by the company.
9. Hank Williams
10. Ralph Emery

51. MEL TILLIS

1. Florida
2. Sherry Bryce
3. Love
4. Coca-Cola ("Coca-Cola Cowboy")
5. Heart
6. Johnny Carson
7. Charlie's
8. *Love, American Style*
9. "Entertainer of the Year"
10. Webb Pierce

52. BILL ANDERSON

1. South Carolina
2. *Backstage at the Grand Ole Opry*
3. From the "Po' Boys" to the "Po' Folks"
4. *One Life to Live*
5. "City Lights"
6. Newspaper writer
7. Country Music
8. Liars 1, Believers 0
9. "Still"
10. I Love You

53. JOHNNY CASH

1. Luther Perkins (guitar) and Marshall Grant (bass)
2. "Jackson"
3. A teenage queen
4. Electrical appliance salesman
5. Yes. It is parked in front of Johnny's "House of Cash" in Hendersonville, Tennessee. It was constructed and given to Johnny by a fan.
6. Gunfighters and trains
7. "Five Feet High and Rising"
8. Folsom Prison
9. *The Gunfight*
10. Dr. Winston restored Johnny to complete health in the late 1960's.

145

54. KENNY ROGERS

1. "The Gambler" and "Coward of the County"
2. The New Christy Minstrels
3. Photographer
4. "Ruby, Don't Take Your Love to Town"
5. Kim Carnes
6. Songwriter
7. "Lucille"
8. "Lady"
9. *Hee Haw*
10. "All I Ever Need Is You"

55. ERNEST TUBB

1. Andrews Sisters
2. He shows the audience the backside of his guitar on which the word "Thanks" is written.
3. Carnegie Hall in New York City
4. Record shop
5. Loretta Lynn
6. Jimmie Rodgers
7. Movies
8. He was elected to the Country Music Hall of Fame.
9. "Walkin' the Floor Over You"
10. "Missing in Action"

146

56. EDDY ARNOLD

1. Tennessee
2. "Entertainer of the Year"
3. "Any Time"
4. "Cattle Call"
5. RCA
6. "I'll Hold You in My Heart"
7. Farming (hence the nickname "Tennessee Plowboy")
8. Log Cabin syrup
9. "Texarkana Baby"
10. He has been on the charts in every decade since the 1940's.

57. RONNIE MILSAP

1. North Carolina
2. Ham radio
3. "Entertainer of the Year"
4. "Any Day Now"
5. Lawyer
6. "I Hate You"
7. Jim Reeves
8. "Daydreams About Night Things"
9. "What a Difference You've Made in My Life"
10. "20/20 Vision"

58. MARTY ROBBINS

1. Arizona
2. El Paso
3. *Marty Robbins Spotlight*
4. Race car driving
5. So he could set the clock back and stay on stage longer
6. Western (with a Mexican influence)
7. Songwriter
8. "Singing the Blues"
9. They are titles of films Marty has starred in.
10. The last "Grand Ole Opry" show at the Ryman Auditorium

59. STATLER BROTHERS

1. Virginia
2. A facial tissue box
3. "Flowers on the Wall"
4. Randolph Scott
5. "Class of '57"
6. The Kingsmen
7. Country star
8. Old local and live country music radio shows
9. July 4—the Statlers present their annual free benefit show in Staunton, Virginia.
10. Johnny Cash

60. KITTY WELLS

1. Nashville
2. *Louisiana Hayride*
3. Johnny Wright
4. First female to have a #1 country hit on the *Billboard* charts
5. Voted into the Country Music Hall of Fame
6. They all recorded duets with Kitty.
7. "Amigo's Guitar"
8. "Heartbreak U.S.A."
9. Three
10. "Making Believe"

61. DONNA FARGO

1. North Carolina
2. English
3. "Happiest Girl in the U.S.A."
4. "Funny Face" and "Superman"
5. It was voted CMA "Single of the Year"
6. Songwriter
7. "U.S. of A."
8. "Mockingbird Hill"
9. The Pony Express
10. "You Can't Be a Beacon If Your Light Don't Shine"

62. TOM T. HALL

1. Kentucky
2. "Harper Valley P.T.A."
3. "Mr. Bojangles"
4. "Salute to a Switchblade"
5. "The Year That Clayton Delaney Died"
6. Beer
7. Watermelon Wine
8. "Fox on the Run"
9. A monkey
10. Love
    Ruby
    Country

63. BARBARA MANDRELL

1. Texas
2. He was a drummer in the Mandrell family band.
3. Five-string banjo, steel guitar, saxophone, bass, and guitar
4. NBC
5. "Female Vocalist of the Year"
6. Saudi Arabia
7. "Sleepin' Single in a Double Bed"
8. Her dad, Irby Mandrell
9. Irlene and Louise
10. of Strangers
    by a Feeling
    Married but

64. WILLIE NELSON

1. Texas
2. Ray Price
3. Charley Pride
4. "Crazy"—Patsy Cline; "Hello Walls"—Faron Young; and "Night Life"—Ray Price
5. Movie acting
6. The "Outlaw"
7. His July 4 outdoor festivals in Texas
8. Tompall, Jessi Colter, and Waylon Jennings
9. "Heartbreak Hotel"
10. Lefty Frizzell; "To Lefty from Willie"

65. WHO AM I?

Answer to all questions: Faron Young

66. DON WILLIAMS

1. Texas
2. Pozo-Seco Singers
3. *W. W. and the Dixie Dancekings*
4. "Amanda"
5. "Male Vocalist of the Year"
6. Because of his ability to correct weaknesses in songs
7. Jeans, jean jacket, shirt, and his ever familiar cowboy hat
8. "The Shelter of Your Eyes"
9. "You're My Best Friend"
10. to the Radio
    Rivers All Run Dry
    Time

67. RAY PRICE

1. Texas
2. Farming or ranching
3. *Big D Jamboree*
4. Hank Williams's Driftin' Cowboys
5. Roger Miller
6. Seventeen violins from the Nashville Symphony
7. "I Won't Mention It Again"
8. "Crazy Arms"
9. Drums
10. Keep Walking Back To You
    by the Number

68. PATSY CLINE

1. Virginia
2. Arthur Godfrey's *Talent Scouts*
3. "Walkin' After Midnight"
4. 1973
5. "I Fall to Pieces"
6. *Coal Miner's Daughter*
7. "She's Got You"
8. "Have You Ever Been Lonely"
9. "Always"
10. Dreams of You
    Faded
    on Your Mind

69. JIM REEVES

1. Texas
2. St. Louis Cardinals
3. Abbott Records
4. *Kimberly Jim*
5. *Louisiana Hayride*
6. Jim's widow Mary
7. "Mexican Joe"
8. It crossed over onto the pop charts
9. Deborah Allen
10. Yonder Comes a
    I Losing
    Drums

70. HANK WILLIAMS

1. Alabama
2. Jimmie Rodgers
3. George Hamilton
4. Hank Williams, Jr.
5. MGM and Fred Rose
6. "I Saw the Light"
7. "I'll Never Get Out of This World Alive"
8. They were the very first to be voted into the Country Music Hall of Fame
9. "I'm So Lonesome I Could Cry"
10. Move/Over
    the Foods on Fire
    These Chains from My Heart
    as

71. HANK SNOW

1. Nova Scotia
2. "I'm Movin' On"
3. Films, notably B westerns
4. Rhinestones
5. Prevention of child abuse
6. RCA
7. Kelly Foxton
8. "I've Been Everywhere"
9. Jimmie Rodgers
10. Rhumba
    Makin' Mama from
    Don't Hurt

72. DOLLY PARTON

1. Tennessee
2. Porter Wagoner
3. Her personal life as one of twelve children born to a mountain family
4. "Entertainer of the Year" and "Female Vocalist of the Year"
5. Fired her band and management firm, striking out with new people to guide her career in a new, more encompassing direction
6. Monument Records
7. It was her first #1 hit record on *Billboard*'s charts.
8. Jane Fonda and Lily Tomlin
9. "Coat of Many Colors"
10. Is Like a
    I Can Do
    Two/Down

73. LORETTA LYNN

1. Kentucky
2. Butcher Hollow
3. Wilburn Brothers
4. "Honky Tonk Girl" on Zero Records
5. Hurricane Mills, Tennessee
6. "Don't Come Home A-Drinkin' "
7. "Vocal Duo," with Conway Twitty
8. Frank Sinatra
9. "Coal Miner's Daughter"
10. Lookin' at
    Fist
    on the Way
    Is the
    in Paradise

74. CONWAY TWITTY

1. Mississippi
2. "It's Only Make Believe"
3. They are the names of movies Conway starred in during his rock 'n' roll years.
4. "Next in Line" (*Billboard* #1)
5. c.
6. Two towns: Conway in Arkansas and Twitty in Texas
7. Twitty City
8. Twittybird
9. None! (Surprising, eh?)
10. Hello
    Fifteen years
    Tight Fittin'

75. CHARLEY PRIDE

1. Mississippi
2. "All I Have to Offer You (Is Me)"
3. Picking cotton
4. "Kaw-Liga"
5. Male Vocalist of the Year (1971 and 1972)
6. "Entertainer of the Year"
7. "A Whole Lotta Things to Sing About"
8. RCA
9. Henry Mancini
10. Take a Little Bit Longer
    Jamaica
    Fries

76. BUCK OWENS

1. Texas
2. Studio back-up musician
3. Rose Maddox
4. Bakersfield
5. "Act Naturally." It was Buck's first #1 *Billboard* hit.
6. *Hee Haw*
7. Bandsman Don Rich (now deceased) won for "Instrumentalist of the Year" in 1974 and the entire band won "Instrumental Group of the Year" in 1967 and 1968.
8. A tiger
9. *Music City News*
10. Tall
    Under/Again
    Together

77. WAYLON JENNINGS

1. Texas
2. The late Buddy Holly
3. "Male Vocalist of the Year"
4. Willie Nelson
5. James Garner (and he sang, too!)
6. Luckenbach, Texas
7. Anita Carter
8. "This Time"
9. Hank Williams ("Are You Sure Hank Done It This Way") and on the other side, Bob Wills ("Bob Wills Is Still the King")
10. Hearted Woman
    Come/Me
    Been Crazy

78. LYNN ANDERSON

1. North Dakota
2. "Listen to a Country Song"
3. "Female Vocalist of the Year"
4. Horseback riding and training
5. Liz Anderson
6. Lawrence Welk
7. "Rocky Top"
8. "Cry"
9. "What a Man My Man Is"
10. My Man
    Can I Unlove You
    of the World

79. MICKEY GILLEY

1. Louisiana
2. "Room Full of Roses"
3. Jerry Lee Lewis
4. *Urban Cowboy*
5. Mechanical bull riding
6. "True Love Ways" and "Stand By Me"
7. "I Overlooked an Orchid"
8. Barbi Benton
9. *The Fall Guy*, starring Lee Majors
10. the Girls All Get Prettier at Closing
    Honky Tonk
    Overnight

80. TAMMY WYNETTE

1. Mississippi
2. She was a beautician.
3. Epic Records
4. First female to sell a million records
5. "Apartment #9"
6. "I Don't Wanna Play House" (*Billboard* #1)
7. "D-I-V-O-R-C-E"
8. "We're Gonna Hold On" (*Billboard* #1)
9. "Near You"
10. I Can Make It on My Own
    Loves Me All the Way
    Woman/Woman

81. MERLE HAGGARD

1. California
2. As governor of California, Reagan pardoned Haggard from his prison sentence.
3. Record producer Tom Collins
4. Bonnie Owens
5. Trains
6. Clint Eastwood
7. "Okie from Muskogee"
8. Bob Wills ("For the Last Time")
9. "From Graceland to the Promised Land"
10. a Great Afternoon
    We Make It Through December
    I'll Just Stay Here and Drink

82. SONNY JAMES

1. Alabama
2. "Young Love"
3. Lon Chaney, Jr.
4. Sixteen consecutive #1 records on the *Billboard* charts
5. He has taken previously recorded songs and done them in his distinctive style to make them hits again.
6. He doesn't sing on it. He plays the guitar.
7. Capitol Records
8. He was born into a show business family.
9. "Take Good Care of Her"
10. Date/Kiss/Love
    Is Wrong With My Baby
    South of Saskatoon

83. WHO AM I?

Answers to all questions: Carl Smith

84. WHO AM I?

I am Glen Campbell.
10. the Everyday Housewife
    on My Mind
    Time I Get to Phoenix

85. GEORGE JONES

1. Texas
2. Starday, Musicor, and Mercury
3. Gene Pitney
4. Melba Montgomery, Margie Singleton, and Brenda Carter
5. "White Lightning"
6. "Single of the Year" (1980)
7. Johnny Paycheck
8. "The Same Old Me"
9. "He Thinks I Still Care," according to several publications
10. Shot Sam
    Bartender's
    Through This World with

86. WHO AM I?

Answer to all questions: Webb Pierce

87. DON GIBSON

1. North Carolina
2. Knoxville, Tennessee
3. "Sweet Dreams"
4. "I Can't Stop Loving You"
5. "Oh Lonesome Me"
6. "(I'd Be) A Legend in My Time"
7. Sue Thompson and Dottie West
8. Blue Blue
9. "I'm Movin' On"
10. Myself a Party
    One Time
    Sensuous Woman

88. OAK RIDGE BOYS

1. Minor league baseball
2. Richard Sterban, Bill Golden, Joe Bonsall, and Duane Allen
3. Gospel
4. "Y'all Come Back Saloon"
5. "Vocal Group of the Year"
6. "Elvira"
7. Chocolate and Chocolate Chip
8. Boy Scouts of America
9. "Bobbie Sue"
10. of Mine
    Leavin'/in the Broad
    Be True to

89. MISCELLANEOUS

1. Rodney Crowell
2. Janie Fricke
3. John Anderson
4. The Kendalls
5. Hoyt Axton
6. George Hamilton IV
7. Skeeter Davis
8. Dickey Lee
9. Terri Gibbs
10. John Conlee

90. MISCELLANEOUS

1. Rex Allen, Jr.
2. Moe Bandy
3. Johnny Paycheck
4. The Gatlins (Larry, Steve, and Rudy)
5. Emmylou Harris
6. Crystal Gayle
7. Alabama
8. Jack Greene
9. Anne Murray
10. Ferlin Husky

91. DAVID HOUSTON

1. Louisiana
2. *Louisiana Hayride*
3. Yodeling
4. They are titles of movies David has appeared in.
5. "Almost Persuaded"
6. Tammy Wynette
7. Tommy Overstreet
8. Robert E. Lee and Sam Houston
9. "Mountain of Love"
10. One Exception
    a Little
    Good

92. JERRY LEE LEWIS

1. Louisiana
2. "Whole Lotta Shakin' Goin' On"
3. *High School Confidential*
4. Othello. Jerry Lee played Iago.
5. "Chantilly Lace"
6. "Middle Age Crazy"
7. "Over the Rainbow"
8. Linda Gail
9. "Great Balls of Fire"
10. Wine Spo-Dee O'Dee
    Gonna Play This Old
    Made/Famous

93. HANK THOMPSON

1. Texas
2. Tex Ritter
3. Songwriting
4. Voted America's #1 western band by nearly every major music trade paper.
5. "On Tap, in the Can, or in the Bottle"
6. "Squaws Along the Yukon"
7. A six-pack
8. "She's Just a Whole Lot Like You"
9. Mills Brothers
10. Sailor
    Violin, the/Music
    the Bar

94. ELVIS

1. "Blue Moon of Kentucky
2. "Baby Let's Play House" (1958)
3. $35,000
4. The Jordanaires
5. *Love Me Tender*
6. Scotty Moore and Bill Black
7. Colonel Tom Parker, Eddy Arnold
8. "I Forgot to Remember to Forget" and its flip side "Mystery Train"
9. "I Really Don't Want to Know" and its flip side "There Goes My Everything"
10. He was only seen from the waist up because of his famous hip gyrations.

95. ROGER MILLER

1. Texas
2. Ray Price
3. *Robin Hood*
4. Roger won six Grammy Awards in 1965.
5. "Husbands and Wives"
6. "King of the Road"
7. They were on both the country and pop charts.
8. It was "Engine Engine #9"
9. Andy Williams
10. Dang
    Roller Skate in a Buffalo
    Dyin'/a Buryin'

96. ROY CLARK

1. Virginia
2. Jimmy Dean
3. National Country Music Banjo Championship
4. Wanda Jackson
5. Hank Thompson
6. Buck Trent
7. "Entertainer of the Year"
8. Lemonade
9. *The Tonight Show Starring Johnny Carson*
10. of My Fingers
    Yesterday When I Was
    God and

97. MISCELLANEOUS

1. Dave Rowland and Sugar
2. Gene Watson
3. Tanya Tucker
4. Eddie Rabbitt
5. George Burns
6. Razzy Bailey
7. Billy "Crash" Craddock
8. Charley McClain
9. Ronnie McDowell
10. Juice Newton

98. WHO AM I?

I am Charlie Rich.
10. Behind/Doors
   Most/Girl
   Won't Be

99. MISCELLANEOUS

1. Hank Williams, Jr.
2. Terry Bradshaw
3. Boxcar Willie
4. Christy Lane
5. Orion
6. Jeanne Pruett
7. Slim Whitman
8. Rosanne Cash
9. Lacy J. Dalton
10. Johnny Duncan

100. MISCELLANEOUS

1. Gary Stewart
2. Brenda Lee
3. Connie Smith
4. Joe Stampley
5. Narvel Felts
6. Bobby Bare
7. Tommy Overstreet
8. Freddy Fender
9. Billie Jo Spears
10. Ronnie Prophet

ANSWERS TO PHOTO QUIZ SECTION

1. "I Dreamed of a Hillbilly Heaven"
2. Queen
3. A yo-yo
4. *The Electric Horseman*
5. The only truly unknown artist to be signed to the show as a regular
6. The Blue Boys
7. *The Laughing Man of Woodmont Cove*
8. His famous dad, Hank Williams
9. Roy Clark
10. Red Sovine
11. Crisco
12. Mel has written songs recorded by each artist.
13. Pasadena, Texas

14. On dozens of radio and television commercials
15. The Gentle Giant
16. False. He's entertained in prison, but never served time in one.
17. "Any Day Now"
18. Emmylou Harris
19. "Midnight Hauler"
20. Porter Wagoner

BIBLIOGRAPHY

Brooks, Tim, and Earle Marsh. *The Complete Directory to Prime Time Network TV Shows 1946–Present.* New York: Ballantine Books, 1979.

Dellar, Fred, *The Illustrated Encyclopedia of Country Music.* New York: a Salamander Book published by Harmony Books, 1977.

Shelton, Robert, and Bert Goldblatt. *The Country Music Story.* New York: Bobbs-Merrill, 1966.

Stambler, Irwin, and Grelun Landon. *Encyclopedia of Folk, Country and Western Music.* New York: St. Martin's Press, 1969.

Whitburn, Joel. *Record Research Top Country & Western Records 1949–1977* and *Top Country Singles & LPs 1978, 1979, 1980 and 1981.* (published privately by author)

About the Author
Dennis Hazzard is program director of country music radio station WAFL-FM, Milford, Delaware. He instructs a course in the fundamentals of broadcasting for Delaware Technical and Community College, manages a bus tour operation for WAFL Radio, and produces an annual country music talent competition for the Delaware State Fair that attracts contestants from a four-state area. He developed his appreciation for country music when, as a teenage disc jockey in the late 1950's, he hosted a show on radio called "Music Country Style."